THE TRAD ARCH. HANDBOOK

A PRACTICAL GUIDE

by
Hilary Greenland

FOURTH EDITION
Revised and Enlarged

Printed by Sylvan Archery, Bristol, England.
First printed November 1993
Revised Edition November 1994
Third Edition 1996
Fourth Edition December 2001
Reprint January 2004
Reprint February 2009
ISBN 0 9524627 6 1

*This book is dedicated to the many archers and craftsmen
who have shared their knowledge, their good company and
sense of humour with me over the years, and –most of all– to
archers throughout the world who keep the spirit of true
archery tradition alive.*

Also available
GERMAN EDITION ISBN 978-3-938921-06-07
FRENCH EDITION ISBN 3-9805877-3-8
Verlag Angelika Hörnig

SYLVAN ARCHERY

No. 4 TA6 4TF
England

CONTENTS

Notes on the Fourth Edition
Introduction (First Edition)

1. **What type of bow?**   1
     The English longbow
     The American flatbow (American longbow)
     The recurve
     Primitive bows
     The archer's paradox
     Gap shooting

2. **Ordering/selecting your bow**   9
     English longbow
     American longbow (flatbow)
     Recurve
     Primitive bows: definition

3. **The master eye**   17

4. **Tuning**   18
     Matching arrows to bow
     Bracing height/strings
     Nocking point
     Arrow fit to string
     Other equipment: adjustment and care
     Troubleshooting

5. **Arrows**   24
     Spining shafts
     Making a spinetester
     Cutting/shaping feathers
     Types of arrow and their uses
     Types of arrowheads and fletchings
     Making a set of matched arrows
     Footed shafts/self nocks
     Flight arrows: making

6. **Strings**   50
     Types of string & materials
     How to make a laid in string
     Serving

7. **Care of your bow**   59

8. Making a primitive bow   64
    Wood, materials and tools
    Cutting dimensions
    Backings
    Tillering
    Finishing
    Cutting dimensions:
        English longbow
        American longbow (flatbow)
        'Pyramid' bow

9. More historic bow designs   89
    Seasoning and splitting billets
    Some historic & prehistoric bow designs
    Cutting dimensions
        Meare Heath type
        Cable backed bow
        Holmegaard style

10. Making a thumbring   101

Glossary of terms   104

Useful data/reference   112
    Conversion/units of length/weight
    Specifications (based on British Long-Bow Society Rules):
        English longbow
        Standard Arrow
    Timber terms

Index

INSTINCTIVE ARCHERY

This book is mainly intended for those interested in traditional English longbows, flatbows, primitive bows, self bows, and hunting-style recurves, and who literally shoot barebow, i.e. without any sight or stabilising attachment on their bow. 'Instinctive shooting' refers to the technique of shooting without any sights, the main style adopted being to anchor the draw at the side of the face, and to shoot with a canted bow.

NOTES ON THE FOURTH EDITION

When I first started this Handbook some years ago it was intended to be a foundation book for all those who were interested in taking up traditional archery, the intention being to gather together in one place information I had gleaned from many sources –written as well as anecdotal, listening to experienced traditional archers and putting this information and some ideas of my own to the test.

Over the years I have found that there is so much to Traditional Archery that you never stop learning; whether you are interested in the history, technology, craft or shooting skills of this fascinating subject, there is a whole world of archery out there waiting to be discovered. As a result this book has grown somewhat over the years, as has the interest in the subject worldwide.

While I hope the information here will present a good start for those new to the subject, I think there is now more to this new edition than the basics, and I'd like to thank those archers who have shared their views, information and advice on what to add and clarify, in particular those who have encouraged me to keep working and experimenting and so to publish this expanded and revised edition of the handbook.

Most important of all, I have discovered over the years since I started out on this adventure, that shooting in good company with a trusty bow which has also become your friend is one of the most enjoyable ways of spending time that there is!

Hilary Greenland
Bristol, England.
November 2001

ORIGINAL INTRODUCTION
(to the First Edition 1993)

The 'traditional' archer has been somewhat neglected over recent years; mainstream archery has become the province of 'high-tech' bows with the sights, stabilisers and associated equipment needed to achieve the high scores expected in target archery nowadays. The invention of compound bows has resulted in a preoccupation with perfect scores and high arrow speeds (just read some of the adverts for the latest compounds if you want to see what I mean).

However, there has been a small band of archers who have kept the spirit of old-time archery alive, and whose efforts have assisted today's revival of the simpler forms of the sport. Increased interest in these traditions (particularly shooting in the English longbow) is gratifying for those who have, for years, extolled the virtues of simplicity in archery.

Most traditional archers want to go beyond just the shooting –they wish to know more about the colourful history of archery and its associated crafts. Many are very individualistic and wish to personalise their kit. While this approach to archery is not the sole province of the traditional archer, there is a world of difference between making a wooden shafted arrow (a skill which most traditionalists learn), and putting together an aluminium shaft with plastic vanes. There are some fine bowyers, fletchers and leatherworkers among the ranks of traditional archers.

The information in this book has been gleaned from chatting to experienced archers, and from making the equipment myself for some years. Doubtless some people will criticise, and can improve on the advice I've set out –what works for one person does not necessarily suit another. All I can say is, keep your ears and eyes open when around experienced traditional archers and make up your own mind. You will soon find out who talks sense! This is an attempt to provide a useful, single, comprehensive source specifically aimed at the traditional archer who is just 'starting out'; as such, it is intended as a guide to the basics only. The rest is up to you.

Good luck, and good shooting,

Hilary Greenland   Bristol
October 1993.

1. WHAT TYPE OF BOW?

WHAT IS A TRADITIONAL BOW?

The 'instinctive' shooting style as described at the start of this book is an essential part of the traditional side of archery and its meaning is well understood, as is the 'traditional' arrow with its wooden shaft and natural feather fletchings –but defining what constitutes a traditional bow can be contentious. In my view the term applies to any bow which conforms to all of the following:

– it has a timber riser, with natural materials (e.g. wood, horn, bone. sinew) forming the major part of the working limbs.

– it is shot in the 'instinctive' (literally 'barebow') style, i.e. it has no sights, stabilisers or pressure buttons.

– it does not rely on wheels, cams, cables etc. to enhance performance (i.e. it depends on the limb design and materials used for its cast and character).

AN OUTLINE OF BOW TYPES

Having decided to shoot a traditional bow, not only does the archer have to choose which particular type to shoot, but also he or she has to select one from a bewildering array of goods on offer from archery suppliers and bowyers. Many new archers change their bows within the first six months; sometimes they choose a bow with a different draw weight as their style and skill develops, but frequently they decide to change the type (or 'class') of weapon. Below is an attempt to outline the characteristics of the main types of traditional bow currently on offer, which may help the novice traditional archer make a decision.

1. The English Longbow

The history and romance of this famous weapon is well documented elsewhere so I will stick to the practicalities. This is a comparatively difficult bow to shoot accurately and consistently, so most longbow archers make this choice for reasons other than getting high scores! An English longbow's performance and 'feel' is determined by the wood from which it is made as well as the skills of the maker, so each bow has its own character. The overall mass and simple design of the 'straight staved' longbow makes it less efficient in relation to draw weight than other types of bow, so it is said to have relatively poor 'cast' when compared with other designs. The famed achievements of mediaeval archers arose from their skills, strength and military deployment, rather than the mechanical efficiency of their bows, but it is the very simplicity of the English longbow which makes it so special to many archers.

Variations on the theme

The straight-staved bow which has been named the 'English longbow' is generally considered to be the typical mediaeval design (as used for the historic 'war bow'). One major advantage of the narrow 'D' section of the longbow is that more staves can be obtained from a good quality yew billet than with wider-limbed designs, which was ideal for mass-production of straight-staved bows for military use in the mediaeval and Tudor period. There are several forms of the 'D' section longbow, including an elegant style pictured in several 15th century English paintings where the ends of the limbs are reflexed away from the archer. Reflexed/deflexed laminated composite longbows, very similar in design to some modern American longbows, were also contemporaries of the straight-staved bow in Europe. The technical advantages of recurving the limbs are discussed later in this chapter, and while the variants described have better shooting characteristics than the straight staved longbow, they still shoot around a relatively wide handle. The following is an attempt to explain why such designs are more difficult to shoot with the same degree of accuracy and consistency than other designs with narrower handles.

The archer's paradox

Because of the width of the handle, the arrow has to travel around the bow; the illustration on the opposite page shows how the shaft has to flex in order to clear the bow; this is a function of the following:
   – arrow spine
   – bow draw weight
   – width of bow section where the arrow passes
   – the action of the string 'rolling' off the fingers
   – the archer's technique (a good loose helps a lot!)
This action has been named the 'archer's paradox', and in order for the arrow to clear the bow and go where it is pointed it must be correctly spined for the bow. The principles of the archer's paradox apply to most bows –although rather less with the really heavy draw weights– but it's effect is most noticeable with bows having a wide handle.

'Modern' answers

Modern flatbows and recurves usually have arrow shelves or sight windows (cutaways) which allow the arrow to pass closer to the centre of the bow, so reducing the paradox; as a result the arrow loses less energy in flight and cast is improved. A bow that is close to centre-shot also has the added benefit of being more forgiving of an archer's inconsistencies!

NOTE: Some archers are discouraged from shooting in the English longbow because they've heard stories of their habit of breaking at full draw, 'topping and tailing' the poor archer in charge of it. This doesn't happen often, and there should be no need for you to purchase a tin hat or archer's box if you observe basic and sensible guidelines regarding selection of the right bow, and take good care of it during and between shoots.

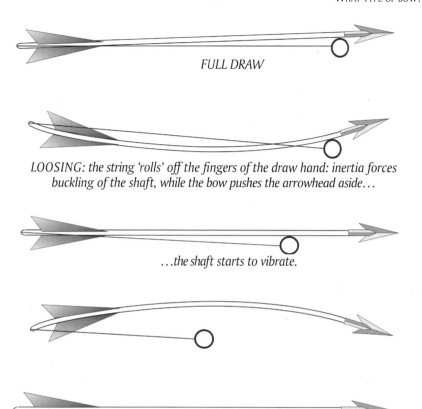

FULL DRAW

LOOSING: the string 'rolls' off the fingers of the draw hand: inertia forces buckling of the shaft, while the bow pushes the arrowhead aside...

...the shaft starts to vibrate.

The vibration must be correct for the shaft to flex past the bow correctly. The arrow is rotating and flexing simultaneously.

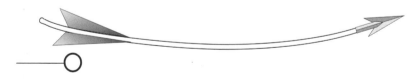

The arrow, having cleared the bow, must straighten as soon as possible in order to maintain accurate and efficient flight.

THE ARCHER'S PARADOX
(Right handed archer)

3

2. The American flatbow (AFB/ American longbow)

The pre-fibreglass American flatbow is a hybrid between the English longbow and shorter wider-limbed bows of native American tribes who made bows of various designs according the materials available, these included horn, sinew and many species of timber which are still popular with today's traditional bowmakers: Osage orange, yew, mulberry, black locust and ash among them. Most tribes used flat, rectangular limb sections (although the Cherokee longbow is similar to the 'English' design); they often applied sinew backings in order to improve cast and reliability, particularly on the shorter bows.

GRP Laminations

Resin laminations with a high unidirectional glass-fibre content were specifically developed for bowmaking, resulting in the predominance of GRP clad flatbows seen in this class today; these bows have a number of mechanical advantages over the traditional, deeper profiled English longbow:

– the GRP reinforcement improves reliability, increases cast and allows a shorter, faster bow to be made

– in the correct proportions the combination of the wood core and GRP laminations produces a 'sweeter' shooting bow. The type, taper and proportions of the wood core contribute to the bow's 'feel' and performance

– the reinforced handle can be cut closer to centre, thus reducing the effects of the paradox. This generally means that the bow is more forgiving of errors in technique than the English longbow.

The American longbow with a narrow handle is also a little more tolerant of mismatches in equipment and tuning, but to be a first class shot correctly matched equipment is essential –good archers will spend some time 'tuning' and matching their kit. (See chapter 4)

Not quite that simple...

Alternatives to the 'straight-limbed' flatbow have been developed in an attempt to improve the characteristics of the bow; some bowyers specialise in bow experimentation, particularly in the USA, and a wide range of flatbows with various limb curvatures, profiles and cross-section are now available. The two main variations on the American longbow–deflex and deflex/reflex– are illustrated later.

3. The Recurve

This type of bow has a worldwide history going back thousands of years, the short composite bows of the Far East being the most well known. Native American tribes recurved and backed their short wood bows ; rawhide, sinew, horn and bone have been used for many centuries as backings to improve a bow's performance and durability; in modern 'high-

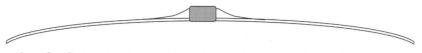

The reflex flatbow has improved cast, but can be more critical to shoot than its straight limbed counterpart

The deflex/reflex flatbow is intended to improve cast with reduced handshock

tech' bows these have been superseded by GRP or carbon-fibre laminations. Recurved bows from China, India and Korea are all well documented, and unlike the longbows of the Middle Ages, fine examples still exist for study today. The popular short hunting-style recurves of the 1960's gave way to the compound bows and longer 'take-down' recurves as seen in most target competitions nowadays, but modern versions of classic designs such as the short Asian composite bows incorporating GRP laminations and large working recurves are now available for the instinctive shooter with a sense of adventure!

There are two types of recurve:

    – the '**working**' recurve unbends as you come to the end of the draw
    – the '**static**' recurve remains stiff at full draw.

Recurves reduce the string angle at full draw, improving leverage, and reducing the 'stacking' effect of a shorter bow. Shorter bows are generally faster, pound for pound, than the equivalent longer bow due to reduced mass and a more rapid limb recovery. Most commercially available recurves have a working recurve, including short (50 inch) Korean style bows with large radius recurves and short riser which are remarkably sweet to draw. A variation on the static recurve is the short bow with stiffened 'ears' (Turkish '*siyahs*') at the limb ends –an historic design from Asia which is now popular in the West; these bows often have glassfibre in the limbs because the genuine article made of horn and sinew requires a great degree of skill and time to make, and needs considerable care by the archer to maintain it's shooting qualities.

4. Other traditional bow designs

With the growth of interest in worldwide archery there are a number of bow designs available which approximate traditional and historic designs: most use glassfibre in lieu of original sinew, horn and wood combinations; some use wood cores with glass fibre laminations on the back and belly. Generally speaking solid glassfibre limbs are heavy in hand and, all else being equal, they can perform less well than wood/glassfibre composites.

5

'PRIMITIVE' BOWS: A DEFINITION

Concise definition of 'primitive' bows can be a matter of debate: purists prefer that only natural materials be used for any part of the bow's construction, disallowing epoxy resin glues modern finishes or Dacron strings. Event organisers often want a more prosaic definition for use in competition. Assisting the bow's longevity by using modern glues, varnishes and more resilient string material ought to be acceptable –after all, recreational archers nowadays do not always have the same amount of time to cosset their bow as the professionals had in days of old.

A realistic specification for a 'primitive' class of bow should include the following:

– the bow shoots around the handle, with no step, rest or shelf to support the arrow other than the archer's hand.

– that the bow's design puts it outside the British Long-Bow Society's specification for the English longbow. (See 'Useful Data')

– the bow's limbs are made from natural materials which can include horn, sinew, natural fibres and bone.

– modern glues or string materials are acceptable provided they do not radically affect the bow's performance. (e.g. Kevlar strings would be excluded).

Within this outline, subclasses for recurves, certain types of composites and prehistoric styles would be possible.

For those interested in making their own primitive bow, information and cutting dimensions for some designs are included in chapter 9.

A WORD ABOUT BOW WINDOWS

Traditional hunting-style recurves have a short bow window because the average hunting shot is rarely in excess of 40 yards and sights aren't generally used. Longer sight windows have became the norm amongst most modern recurve bow manufacturers in order to maintain the target/sight relationship for the longer distances.

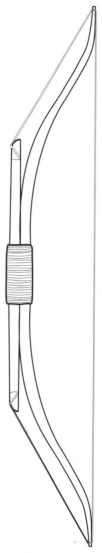

The double 'Penobscot bow' is an advanced 'primitive' design. One example is 60inch long, (possibly made for a 22-24in draw)

'Gap shooters' and 'instinctives'

A truly instinctive archer will shoot an arrow without conscious thought or taking aim –as naturally as throwing a ball, in fact –no calculation of distances or points of aim are involved. By contrast gap-shooters use parts of the bow's riser (e.g. the edges of the cutaway) as an elementary form of sight, while others use the pile of the arrow. I have illustrated the principles of gap-shooting over the page, using the edge of the cutaway which forms the sight window as an example; you can see from this how the pile of the arrow can also be used.

SO HOW DO YOU DECIDE?

Many archers have several types of bow and shoot them all very well. It has to be said, though, that the top archers stick with one particular weapon for some time in order to master it. I will just add a couple of thoughts, which might help. . .

    – if high scores and consistently hitting the target are essential to your mental health, perhaps the English longbow or primitive bow is not for you

    – some competitions are exclusive to the English longbow, for example 'Roving marks', and British Long-Bow Society target and clout meetings, so you may decide to obtain a longbow in order to enjoy these.

Finally...

I would recommend that those of you just starting out begin with a 'training bow' to familiarise yourself with shooting; you need to develop a consistent style before you spend your hard-earned cash on bows which are more difficult to shoot accurately, and which can be less forgiving of mistakes in both shooting and care. Get some good advice on technique (and safety) from an experienced traditional archer. You may even be lucky enough to find one who will provide a suitable bow –I've found most traditional archers are very keen to help the beginner. A GRP backed American longbow or recurve is a good start. When my longbow style has fallen apart in the past, I found a temporary return to shooting with a modern recurve an excellent way of re-establishing a good foundation for all shooting; it makes me re-think my style and technique, so I feel it is a good idea to always have one in the house!

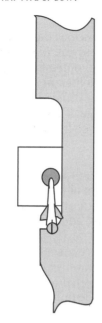

POINT
BLANK

GAP SHOOTING

If you are not a true 'instinctive' and shoot recurve with a cutaway, you may wish to try 'gap shooting' using the edge of the bow's sight window to help with aiming.

Firstly you should determine the 'point blank' range of your bow, and then, with continuous practice, assess the proportion (x) of your sight window which coincides with specific distances to the target. It is then a matter of developing a skill for assessing unmarked distances —which usually means plenty of practice.

If you do not have a sight window cut into your bow, you could use a profile change in the bow near the handle, or the tip of the arrow in the same way.

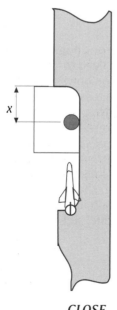

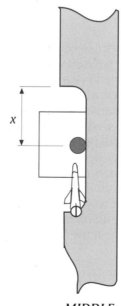

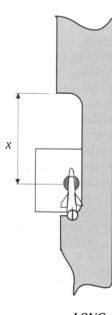

x

x

x

CLOSE
RANGE

MIDDLE
RANGE

LONG
RANGE

2.ORDERING/SELECTING YOUR BOW

ENGLISH LONGBOW

A longbow is a very personal thing. I would no more buy a longbow 'off the peg' than I would purchase a set of second-hand false teeth, because I'd have no idea where it has been, or what has been done with it. If, however, you cannot wait to get your hands on a longbow, some archery shops do have a limited stock, and if you bear in mind the guidelines set out below you may find a suitable bow; remember –the way a longbow has been treated is vital to its longevity and performance.

A good longbow will not have a large degree of 'set' (string follow) in the limbs.
Different woods will take a different degree of set, and good bows can straighten a little when rested correctly. A small degree of set is not a problem and can even make a bow sweeter to shoot. ('Rule of thumb' says set should not be more than 2 inches)

The nocks will be neat and smooth.
Nock shapes are largely a matter of preference, and each bowmaker has a preferred design which can be a personal trademark. The grooves should be deep enough to hold the string but shallow enough to permit easy unstringing; areas where the string makes contact should be smooth and polished, with no sharp edges.

The finish should be suitable.
If you are likely to be shooting over rough terrain in bad weather, a suitably tough finish will be necessary: check with the retailer and get advice on what degree of maintenance the finish requires.

Ensure it complies with the English Longbow specification.
(See Glossary for an outline of the British Long-Bow Society spec.)
This includes rules for drawlength to bow length ratio, type of bow nock allowable for style of competition etc., but –most importantly– consistent limb profile: built-up handles which form a type of arrow rest, or narrowing of limbs at the handle to reduce the effects of the paradox, do not comply with the traditional principles of English longbow design.

I recommend above all that you have your longbow made to order from an experienced bowyer; a list of members belonging to the Craft Guild of Traditional Bowyers and Fletchers is available from the British Long-Bow Society. Ideally, find a bowyer whose work you have seen and liked and who is recommended to you by experienced archers, then discuss your requirements on a personal basis. If you are unsure what to order, a good bowyer can advise you about all aspects of the longbow and what should suit you –most good bowmakers agree on the salient points.

FINDING A BOWMAKER/ORDERING A BESPOKE LONGBOW

A good, professional, quality bowmaker who takes pride in his or her work will ask a reasonable sum for a bespoke traditional longbow made to your requirements, so it is important that you consider very carefully where you place your order.

Check out the bowyer's order book:

A good bowmaker crafting bows to order may well have a lengthy waiting list (some things *are* worth waiting for). A good quality custom-made bow by definition is not a mass produced item, so I would regard any boast regarding speed of manufacture or how many bows are made in a week with caution. Also be prepared to pay a deposit –professional bowyers need to earn a living too!

Traditional bows are made of materials formed by nature, and shaped by human beings:

An honest bowmaker will admit that longbows can occasionally break and will offer a guarantee. Bear in mind that this relies on the bow being well treated by it's owner, particularly early on in it's shooting career. A good longbow is said to be 7/8 broken at full draw so it will require care in use and storage. (See chapter 7)

The bow should be made for you specifically:

A custom bow should be made to your style and drawlength because it is intended to be shot by you only. The bowmaker should be prepared to discuss your requirements with you in detail. If you are offered a 74 inch long bow when you have a 26 inch draw length, it might be worth looking elsewhere...

YOUR BOW ORDER: WHAT YOU NEED TO KNOW
Bow woods

Good quality yew is still the best material for traditional longbows; it possesses the perfect combination of a sapwood which is superbly strong in tension, naturally bonded to a heartwood which performs excellently under compression. Currently much of the yew for bows is imported from the USA (*Taxus brevifolia*) but it can be difficult to obtain top quality staves, and good quality 'self' yew staves and longbows can command a high price. It is said that the best heavy draw weight bows are made from English yew (*Taxus baccata*) –as with many archery debates, the jury is still out on that one. Most English longbows in use nowadays are laminated and usually have a backing strip of hickory, maple or bamboo; they may incorporate other hardwood laminations to assist with performance and longevity; excellent cast and shooting characteristics are obtained with these bows. Bowyers are always experimenting with different timbers, so there will never be a definitive list of bow woods; timbers used include lemonwood, varieties of boxwood, purpleheart, Osage orange, pequia, false acacia (aka black locust), purpleheart and greenheart –the list is constantly changing with the varying availability of good timber.

Starting out

A beginner should shoot a training bow for a while before ordering a bespoke longbow, as some consistency in shooting is needed before any decisions can be taken on bow specification. Don't rush into this –get assistance from an experienced longbow archer who can help you gather the information which your bowyer requires, this should prevent you making a costly mistake. Listed below are the basic considerations:

1. Draw weight

A big mistake is to be 'overbowed', as a bow with too heavy a draw weight will not only wear you out, it could cause you to injure yourself; you could also develop bad shooting habits –you may raise your bow shoulder, underdraw, or throw your bow arm off line in the struggle to draw it back. Conversely don't buy a bow which is below your ideal draw weight and try to achieve the additional poundage by overdrawing, this is sure to weaken the bow, reduce its cast and eventually break it.

2. Draw length

The bow should be made to suit the archer's draw length, therefore it is important that your shooting style settles down before ordering. Tell your bowyer if you intend to overdraw, e.g. when flight shooting.

3. Bow length

The length of the bow should be suited to the archer's draw length. A longer bow is generally easier to draw back, while shorter bows can be faster-shooting, however this latter advantage may be offset by a tendency to 'stack' more, and unfortunately increased arrow speed can highlight an archer's shooting inconsistencies!

4. Shooting style

A bespoke longbow can be made to take an archer's shooting style into account. For instance an inveterate 'holder' at full draw is not a bowyer's friend because this can break a bow; allowance can be made by ordering a longer bow –please be honest with your bowyer!

5. Left or Right hand

If you have tested for your 'master' or 'dominant' eye (see chapter 3) you will have settled on this; the bowyer will need to know on which side to put the protective arrow plate.

6. Types of competition

The type of competition you expect to enjoy also affects your choice of bow draw weight and length etc., and your bowyer can advise on the best longbow for your purposes. There are several types of competition, run by different organisations; in the British Long-Bow Society Rules of Competition, it is stipulated that for most of their events longbows must have horn nocks and be constructed within specific dimensions relating to section and length. 'Self nocked' longbows are allowed in some competitions but check the rules of the organisation running the shoot for details. You may like to have more than one type of longbow in order to be competitive in all the forms of shooting promoted by the various clubs and organisations, however, with an all-purpose longbow you can at least join in. Most men choose a longbow of around 50lb draw weight, women select one a few pounds under this –what an archer can comfortably manage will vary, bearing in mind the points raised above. Below is an outline of some of types of shooting.

Field shooting

Targets are rarely further than 40 yards away, so a magnificent cast is not generally required –having a bow that is manageable is the most important thing as some shoots take two days, and certain rounds can require 120 very accurate arrows! Your bow must be tough enough to take the rigours of clambering up and down muddy slopes, falling into bushes and tripping over tree roots...

Target shooting

Longbows for target use generally have a lighter draw weight than field or flight bows because more arrows are shot in comparatively quick succession (e.g. 144 for a Double National round) so it can be very tiring if you are overbowed. You can't afford to get tired when consistent accuracy is required, particularly over the longer distances.

Roving Marks

This involves long distance shooting –stakes which form the mark can be up to 260 yards away. A heavier draw weight longbow may be desirable to reach the longer marks, together with types of 'flight' arrow. (See chapter 5). Longbows with 'self' nocks can be accepted at these competitions, but check with the organiser first.

Hoyles

Roving at short distances at natural marks such as tufts of grass. An all-purpose bow is fine for this informal pursuit

'Flight' (distance) competitions

Bows for flight competitions should be as heavy a draw weight (up to 85 lb) as the archer can handle without suffering physical injury. Omitting horn bow nocks will add a little speed. Bows over 85lb become less efficient in relation to the increased poundage due to greater limb mass and the need for a stiffer, heavier arrow to match the bow, and 'stand in' well. A perfect match of arrow to bow is essential and a good, smooth but fast loose. It depends on your competitiveness how far you are prepared to strain yourself –many longbow archers are just happy to 'have a go' and see what distance they can get out of their bow.

Heavy arrow competitions (e.g. BL-BS Standard arrow)
If you wish to shoot heavy 'war' arrows over a decent distance (as in British Long-Bow Society 'Standard Arrow' competitions) a bow just within hernia limits is recommended. To be competitive a draw weight of 100lb is only a starter. A heavy arrow needs a 'push' rather than a 'punch' to achieve distance and you need to be able to draw the bow back the full length of a 'war' arrow fitted with a heavy broadhead or bodkin (a Standard Arrow shaft is over 30 inches) so a longbow over 74 inches in length is recommended. The longer limbs will store more potential energy than a shorter bow and a heavy arrowshaft will absorb more of this energy for flight. Shaft profiles are often modified to assist balance and glide. (see chapter 5 and Useful Data)

LONGBOW TILLER/PROFILE

Longbows can be tillered to have a variety of profiles at full draw, each having its own characteristics regarding cast, stack and stability; if you have a preference for a particular profile discuss this with your bowyer; your style of shooting and the type of competition you most enjoy may also influence the choice. There are various terms you may hear regarding the properties and types of the English longbow:

War bow: this is the mediaeval style longbow of heavy draw weight which 'comes compass' (see below), intended originally for military use; it will shift heavy (armour piercing) arrows.

Butt bow: the recreational target bow of lighter draw weight, developed as a sporting weapon.

Compass bow: a longbow which 'comes compass' describes an arc at full draw –an ideal profile for heavyweight 'war' bows and flight bows. It is an efficient design, and rumours that all bows which bend through the handle kick in the hand are greatly exaggerated. The yew longbows found on the Tudor warship 'Mary Rose' (which sank in 1545) were 72 to over 80 inches long and would have had this profile at full draw.

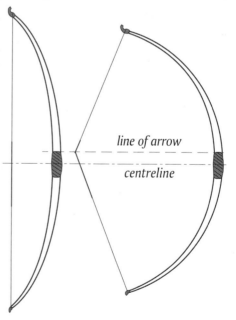

line of arrow

centreline

A longbow which 'comes compass'

Target longbows

Most longbows in use today have what I call the 'target' profile, although I admit this is a misnomer as it makes an excellent all-round bow. Each limb has a stiffened section approx. 6in. above and below the handle which is intended to improve stability. The limb ends are also stiffened; this profile was much favoured by Horace Ford who introduced the principles of all modern target archery in his classic book "Archery: its Theory and Practice", which was first published in 1856.

Buchanan, a bowyer in the middle of the 19th century, introduced the 'dips' seen on

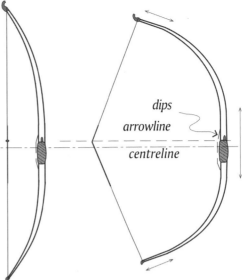

A 'target' style longbow with stiffened areas of limb. Dips indicated by dotted lines

many target longbows today; these deepen and stiffen the handle section and are intended to increase stability.

The centrelines of longbows can also vary, affecting symmetry in string length above and below the nocking point; many bows which 'come compass' have a centreline at the mid point of the handle, i.e. both limbs are the same length. The conventional 'target' longbow usually has a centreline about 1 to 1 1/2 inch above handle centre, this means that the lower limb is shorter and because it is under greater stress, it is usually made stronger than the upper limb. (See chapter 8)

A longbow may combine several features from those I have outlined, to varying degrees according to the tiller, purpose and performance required as well as the materials used. A bowyer may also have a personal preference for a particular tillered profile, having found it most suitable for the way he works.

AMERICAN LONGBOW/FLATBOW (AFB) with GRP laminations

The basics are similar to those for the English longbow, although there is not such a diversity of competition for this type of bow in the UK, so a single all-purpose bow to suit your draw length and style will be fine. There are several makes of AFB now available from bowyers and dealers with a variety of fibreglass colours and core woods. Most off-the-shelf bows have maple cores; bowyers will make to order using other bow woods, including attractive decorative hardwood risers.

RIGHT: Another design of longbow with 'whipped round' (recurved) limbs; this style appears in English paintings from the 15th century onwards.

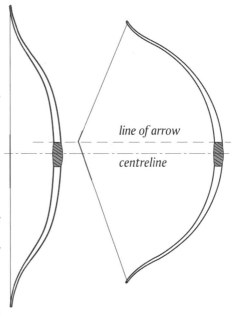

line of arrow

centreline

Factors affecting your choice of AFB are very similar to those set out for the longbow:

1. Draw length

The American longbow is usually made shorter than the English longbow, so it will be faster shooting in relation to it's draw weight. A bow of 68in. long between nocks is suitable for draw lengths of 28/29in., shorter bows can be ordered for draw lengths less than this; have a word with the bowyer if you have any doubts. Just remember that a longer bow usually is sweeter to shoot, but may have reduced cast, pound for pound, than a shorter one. Also be honest. Some archers maintain they have a 28in. draw when they only just reach 5ft. in their platform shoes; unless their knuckles are nearly scraping the ground this draw length is unlikely if they have a traditional shooting style, anchoring to the face. What I am saying is do not order a longer flatbow than you need –you will lose potential cast from the bow. Conversely do not order a flatbow that is too short, as it is more likely to stack with a longer draw.

2. Bow weight

For the same reasons as for the English longbow, don't be overbowed.

3. Limb design

Reflexed/deflexed alternatives to the straight-limbed flatbow have already been described in chapter 1: to summarise, the faster the bow, the less 'forgiving' it is ; some designs are very fast for a relatively long bow, but there is usually a trade-off somewhere!

4. Type of grip

Some commercially available flatbows have a 'pistol' grip (i.e. shaped to the hand); this causes some purists to frown as original American longbows had no such shaping to the grip. It is a matter of preference what you choose to shoot unless competition rules dictate otherwise. A pistol grip can help you maintain a consistent hand position.

15

MODERN RECURVE

Basic principles for your choice of recurve are as set out for other types of bow already discussed; make sure you aren't overbowed, for the same reasons. There are many varieties of this type of bow on the market; apart from fibreglass colour and appearance, the main considerations are:

1. Length of bow

The traditional hunting recurve is usually 58 or 60 inches long, shorter than a typical target recurve because the bow window can be reduced in length for shorter distances. While a short bow is faster and makes the bow less unwieldy in the field, it can be more 'critical' to shoot. A shorter bow can stack, although some designs have a large working recurves which help offset this. The acute string angle resulting from a long draw length on a short bow can also create 'pinching', which causes the fingers to touch the arrow and twist it off the rest while drawing up. Short (50 inch)Korean-style recurves are also available.

2. Type of grip

Most modern recurves have a 'pistol' grip which may help the archer maintain a consistent hand position on the bow, but can (according to design) create a high wrist position which you may find tiring over a long shoot unless you practice frequently –yes, you *do* need to be 'match fit' for archery! Some bows have grooves for individual fingers in order to ensure absolute consistency in the hand grip.

3. Length of riser

This can vary greatly, according to the length of sight window (see 1 above). The important thing to note is the limb length –a longer limb is usually 'sweeter' and more forgiving to shoot, but has less cast than a shorter one.

4. Facility for shooting 'off the shelf'

For instinctive shooting you should rest the arrow to as near 'off your hand' as possible, so check the location and depth of the shelf with this in mind, rather than depend on using a separate arrow rest.

TAKE-DOWN (or TAKE-APART) BOWS

In addition to portability, a major advantage of take-down recurves is that their limbs are interchangeable (dependent on types of fixing), so that the draw weight can be increased as the archer's technique improves. There is usually a trade-off in a small loss of performance over a one-piece bow. Some one-piece bows have a take-down counterpart, this may be longer overall due to the extended riser.

WEIGHT-IN-HAND

Some bows have large risers or solid fibreglass limbs which can be quite heavy, so bear in mind that you may have to use your bow all day, possibly over a two day shoot –a bow which is too heavy can tire you, causing some inaccuracies to 'creep' in.

3. MASTER EYE

Whatever style you shoot, for accurate aiming it helps to draw the arrow to your master eye, this will assist the outright beginner as well as those with severe accuracy problems who may not have tested for it!

How to test for your master (or dominant) eye
With both eyes open, focus on a particular object approx. 10 yards away, through an aperture formed by your hands as illustrated below. Still with both eyes open, bring your hands up to your face, maintaining the object in the centre of the aperture at all times. Your hands will automatically come up to your master eye.

Another method of checking for the dominant eye demonstrates it's importance in aiming: with both eyes open, point with your arm at full length to an object about 10 yards away. Without moving your arm, shut one eye, then the other. When your master eye is open, your finger will still point at the selected object, when you close your master eye, your finger will appear to 'jump' off to one side of the object.

In rare cases you may not have a discernible master eye, in which case take your pick. Some archers have to close one eye at full draw because of this problem, but I would point out that we have both eyes to the front of the head which is a great advantage for quickly and easily judging distance; this is a vital skill for shooting on unmarked field courses, (among other things) so keep both eyes open for this purpose at least!

If for some reason you cannot physically handle the bow in the correct hand to suit your master eye, your brain's sighting mechanism can adjust, but this will take a little effort and time: to start with it may help to close your dominant eye when sighting. Some lucky archers shoot equally well using either left or right hand quite instinctively –others learn to do so through practice.

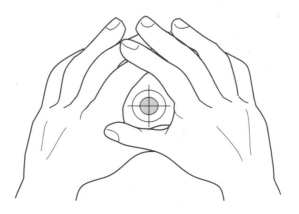

4. TUNING

Tuning?

This is often thought to be a speciality of the high-tech compound bows and target bows with pressure buttons, stabilisers and the like.

Not so!

If you want to hit the mark (and preserve your arrows) you must pay a great deal of attention to 'tuning' traditional bows, because, even if you own a forgiving bow that is centre- or over-centre shot, you need to be sure that your arrows travel around the bow correctly in order that they act consistently and go where they are pointed.

Before I start...

The following may seem at first a complicated approach to traditional archery –after all, the mediaeval English longbowman managed to shoot effectively without the scientific knowledge available to the modern archer, but then he shot in the bow from early childhood and was a trained professional who spent considerable time in practice. The following guidance should give the traditional archer a solid foundation for consistent and accurate shooting, eliminating as many of the variables which can cause those broken arrows and dismal scores. The beauty of shooting a traditional bow is that, having become familiar with it through regular practice, the archer can be more adventurous –after all there are no 'valleys' or drawchecks to cramp your style! Other cultures pay less detailed attention to tuning, but encourage shooting in the bow from a very early age. Experienced instinctive archers can assess an unfamiliar bow setup swiftly and can shoot accurately and consistently after a few initial shots. Those who don't have the opportunity to practice diligently (or have not yet developed a 'natural' talent!) may feel the need for all the help they can get, and the following is essential in this case. It really isn't that complicated, all it takes is a little time and effort but the exercise is fascinating and the rewards are well worth it.

FACTORS IN TUNING

All the main factors involved in tuning your traditional equipment are related to the Archer's Paradox, and they are:

  1. Arrow spine/weight/fletch/length.
  2. Bracing height.
  3. String weight/strand.
  4. Nocking point location.
  5. Correct fit of arrow nock to string.

The above factors are also inter-related, for example, changing bracing height will affect the nocking point location. You may also find that arrows which act badly at a certain bracing height, fly perfectly when this is altered. Ideally you need (or develop through practice) that rare thing, a consistent loose, not only for achieving dream scores but also for testing and tuning your bow.

1. Arrow spine/weight (See also chapter 5)

You must be prepared to spend some time testing arrows with different spined shafts, fletching size and pile weights. Firstly be sure that the arrows are correct for your drawlength –an over-long arrow will fly erratically, too short an arrow is dangerous as it can come inside the bow and shatter. Include shafts of different diameters with the same spine during testing: they will act differently. Matching arrows to bows of low draw weight (below 40lb) can require extra effort due to the degree of flexion required of the shaft to clear the handle. When you find an arrow which comes out well at all distances, record its specifications, weight, spine, fletch and length. so that you can obtain shafts or arrows that are almost identical. Each arrow in a set should also be as closely matched in weight as possible –ideally within 10 grains of each other. (Approx. 15.5grains=1 gramme)

2. Bracing height

This is an important part of tuning your bow. Correct bracing height is not only critical to the longevity of your bow, but is also very important in obtaining a clean, quiet, accurate shot. If your bracing height is too low, several things may happen:

– your arrow will strike the side of the bow
– the arrow will 'wobble' wildly in flight
– you will hit your bracer with an energy-losing 'thwack'
– you will experience hand shock from the bow
– if it is way too far below the recommended limit, you will ultimately break the bow
– a recurve bow will be particularly noisy (although they are often more noisy than a longbow or flatbow).

While a lower bracing height will give the bow more power in relation to draw weight, it may not be good for the bow or for your accuracy. The most efficient bracing height is one which is the lowest you can achieve to shoot cleanly, quietly and consistently, while at the same time being within the design limits of the bow.

FISTMELE
Originally the measure of a clenched fist, this has become specific to archery as a measure of bracing height when the thumb is extended.

The 'fistmele'

Traditionally, longbow bracing height was checked by the 'fistmele' which has come to mean the clenched fist with the thumb extended; I wouldn't depend on this, as there is not a British Standard fistmele in existence. It is better to mark your arrows with the correct distance from nock to the back of the bow, once you have ascertained the best bracing height.

3. The String

The number of strands in the string will affect the potential cast of your bow and its stability in shooting; the fewer strands in the string the faster your bow will shoot. You should not put the bow in danger of breakage by having fewer strands than recommended for its draw weight (see chapter 6), conversely a string which is too thick will be unnecessarily slow. However, a thicker string may well control a bow that is a little too 'critical' for consistency in shooting by slowing it down a tad. When flight shooting you will need a bowstring that is as light as is safe and practicable –that can also include reducing the length of serving (every little helps!) If you do vary the thickness of your strings, it is essential to maintain correct fitting of all your arrow nocks before shooting, not only for good arrow flight but also because a loose nock effectively causes 'dry-loosing' of the bow. Nock which are too tight will cut the string below the serving where you won't see the damage until it's too late.

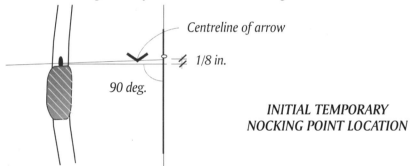

Centreline of arrow

1/8 in.

90 deg.

*INITIAL TEMPORARY
NOCKING POINT LOCATION*

4. Nocking point location

In order to shoot consistently you should have a permanent and hard wearing nocking point which is in the right place. Once your string is 'shot in' and your bracing height correct, set a temporary nocking point so that your arrow nock is approx. 1/8inch above the perpendicular as illustrated. A simple first check is to ask a friend to see if your arrow is close to perpendicular to the riser at full draw when you are shooting (remember not to hold an English longbow at full draw) adjust your nocking point accordingly. This, however, isn't a universal rule, if you have an uneven loose (i.e. your fingers do not all loose the string cleanly) and as long as this is consistent you may find that the nocking point will have to be higher. An incorrectly located nocking point can show itself by the angle of the arrow when it penetrates the target (at short distances), and/or the shaft 'porpoising' in flight; the shaft might graze the knuckle of your bowhand as it 'dips' on release. Firstly make sure these faults aren't caused by any pinching of the arrow with the fingers of the stringhand. Adjust the nocking point gradually, test shooting at various distances; when you are happy that the arrows are consistently flying well apply a permanent hardwearing nocking point. Some people use two built up location points for their nock –most target archers do. For the mediterranean loose in particular I suggest that only the upper nocking point is necessary as the string angle on drawing up will force the arrow nock upward onto the nocking point.

There are several ways of securing a nocking point:

Dental floss
This material is ideal as it is cheap, comes in a handy pack suitable for carrying around with you, and it is tough. Once securely wrapped and tied around the serving a drop of 'superglue' will keep it neat.

Nock-sets
These are metal rings with a rubber lining to prevent string damage, they need a special pliers-type tool to fit and remove. I don't think they belong on a traditional bow.

'Sewing through'
A thin thread (fly-tying thread for example) can be sewn through the serving; this is very hard wearing, but not easily adjusted or removed.

5. Arrow fit to string
Adjusting your nocks to ensure a correct fit to the string is essential to bow survival as well as arrow flight. A nock which is too tight will not only cause arrows to fly badly, but can also cause unseen damage to the string beneath the serving. See the illustration on the opposite page showing adjustment of plastic nocks. A loose nock can mean a dry-loosed (and therefore damaged) bow. If you make your own arrows with self nocks, these should be adjusted correctly; the serving can be built up to provide a secure but not too tight a fit.

ARROW RESTS (Flatbow and recurve)
A traditional instinctive style archer shoots as close to off his hand as possible, as when shooting in the longbow. Some of the cheaper flatbows and recurves have a sloped cutaway that does not form an adequate shelf to support the arrow. There are two solutions to this:
– you build up the shelf with filler/wood/leather so that you can shoot off it
– you elect to use a self-adhesive arrow rest.

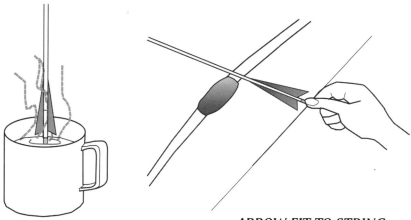

ARROW FIT TO STRING

Nock the arrow onto the string holding the bow so that the arrow hangs vertically. Give the string a sharp, light tap with the side of the fingers –the arrow should drop off the string. If it clings on, or won't stay on the string in the first place, the nock needs to be adjusted.

Plastic nocks can be adjusted by holding them in a cup of hot water until warmed through, then fitting them onto the serving and holding lightly in place until cooled. Recheck the fit as above. If you have to adjust them 'in the field' on no account bite them! Try warming them with the breath and squeezing them between finger and thumb.

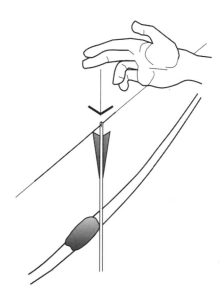

'Self' nocks need workshop attention with sandpaper and file; fit is critical: too tight and you will split the nock which effectively dry-looses the bow. If they are too loose build up the serving at the nocking point.

If you choose the second option, make sure that the rest is substantial enough to take the beating that you will give it shooting relatively heavy wooden arrows 'in the field', some of the fancier wire rests do not last two minutes. It is also a good idea to carry a spare on your person during shoots. Location of the arrow rest is important –keep it as close to your hand as possible, and adjust the arrow/nock angle as described earlier. If you shoot off the shelf you may have to apply a 'plate' of some sort, this protects the bow and can make it more quiet to shoot –it could be a leather pad, thin horn strip or a 'brush rest' of carpet; again, it must be tough enough to take the rigours of traditional shooting.

TABS

When new, some tabs (including those with a spacer between the index and second finger) do not provide sufficient clearance for the arrow and so cause 'pinching' which can push the arrow off the rest while drawing up. Take a sharp knife to the slot and adjust it, then trim the length so that it just covers the fingers. In order to avoid saturation when the British summer does its worst, I have soaked my leather tabs in silicon spray, this resists water and helps keep that essential smoothness for a good, fast release. Always carry a spare tab which has been 'shot in' just in case your old favourite decides to fall apart or lose itself just when you are achieving your all-time greatest score.

SHOOTING GLOVES

These must fit correctly, so be sure to select the right size, make and material from the start. Choose a glove which feels slightly too small at the outset, as it will stretch to fit with use. There are double-seamed and single-seamed varieties, and thickness of material can vary, so (it follows) will the degree of 'feel' or pain you experience! Both shooting gloves and tabs will take a little while to break in from new (like a pair of shoes really). If you carry spares, shoot them in as well.

BRACERS

A wrap-around leather armguard with a leather lace is usual for the traditionalist. Good quality, sturdy leather is recommended, kept nice and smooth on the inside so that the string slips off nicely, should you (inadvertently) hit your arm.

THUMBRINGS

If you have a short recurve or eastern style bow, you might want to try the appropriate loose –the 'thumblock', in which case you will need protection for the thumb. Correct fit of the thumbring is vital: a bad fit can cause a great deal of discomfort as well as affecting the quality of loose. Ideally you should make your own. (See chapter 9)

5. ARROWS

Herein lies the real secret of being a successful archer. An old, tired and twisted bow may shoot well enough to hit the mark if you aim true (up to a point), but even the most perfect bow in the hands of a truly gifted archer will not make up for the problems encountered when shooting unmatched arrows –you may as well resign yourself to raking in the undergrowth. The best way an archer can shoot to the best of his or her ability is to ensure that the equipment is up to it. You will probably find some heated discussion among traditional archers about the best arrows/best fletchings/best weight of pile etc. Find out what works for you and let others know, but be prepared for disagreements!

MATCHED EQUIPMENT
The spine of the arrow should match the bow and the archer's shooting technique and style, because these combine to affect the way an arrow leaves the bow. Needless to say, arrows should be a 'set', matching each other in spine, weight, fletch and pile. All the top archers, whether instinctive or gap-shooters, have matched equipment.

WOODEN SHAFTS
The quality of the arrowshaft and the wood from which it is made is vital for the physical wellbeing of the archer as well as for accuracy –the arrow must be capable of 'standing in' the bow, as an arrow breaking on loosing can be a shattering experience –literally. When selecting the shaft or raw material, ensure that the grain is straight and parallel and has at least two growth rings running the full length of the shaft, with no evidence of resin 'pockets', knots, frets or pins.

Port Orford Cedar /POC *(Chamaecyparis Lawsoniana)*
This has been the fletcher's shaftwood of choice for many years, being strong in relation to it's physical weight; unfortunately good quality inexpensive POC shafts are not easy obtain in quantity in the UK; fortunately there are alternatives –most being heavier than POC. Ash shafts are excellent and very tough, but being relative heavyweights are really only suitable for heavy draw weight bows. Douglas fir, close-grained sitka, hemlock and several varieties of pine can make good shafts.

Making arrowshafts
For those who wish to try their hand at making their own shafts from the square, there follows a descriptive illustration of how to do this; Victorian or Georgian softwood floorboards and cills etc. can make beautiful shafts. If you find suitable timber, it's well worth having a go.

NOTE: arrow wood must be correctly seasoned, if it is too 'green' you will find that the shaft will not straighten properly, and will act more like a rod of putty. A moisture content between 11 and13% should be about right, kiln or air dried. (See also chapters 8 & 9 on seasoning)

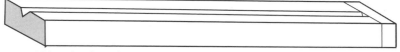

A 'shooting board' with a suitable groove and a stop end facilitates planing the stock

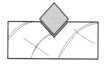  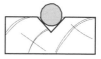

The square stock has the corners/angles progressively planed to form the rounded shaft

Sandpaper

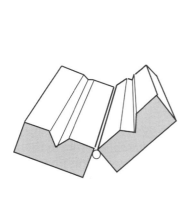 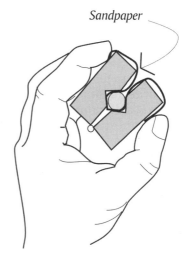

The final rounding and finishing is carried out using a hinged and grooved sanding block.

MAKING SHAFTS FROM THE SQUARE

THE IMPORTANCE OF SPINE
The 'paradox' effect already described means that while arrows have to be sufficiently flexible to clear the bow, they must be sufficiently stiff (and adequately fletched) in order to straighten up quickly thereafter to maintain accurate flight. The spine of an arrow and its success in matching the bow is a function of bow weight, your shooting technique and correct 'tuning' of the bow. (See chapter 4)

25

WHAT IS ARROW SPINE?

The method generally accepted for measuring the spine of wooden arrow shafts is based on the USA (AMO) system. The spine of each arrowshaft is assessed by measuring the amount of deflection it undergoes on the application of a 2lb weight at its mid-point. This usually relates to deflection over a 26 inch length, but I have found one supplier who uses 28 inches –if in doubt, ask– it's important! The shaft is then marked with a poundage which approximates the draw weight of the bow for which it is considered suitable; this, of course, is a bit of a nonsense as all bows are different, but it's the only way wood shafts are categorised at present. Shafts are generally supplied in dozens and are roughly (and it can mean roughly) sorted into 5lb increments. Try and keep your matched set within 0.1in. of each other, preferably .050in. for the heavier bows.

A ROUGH GUIDE TO BOW WEIGHT AND ARROW SPINE

A bow which shoots around the handle (e.g. English longbow) generally requires arrows spined for two-thirds to three-quarters the actual draw weight of the bow at your draw length. A flatbow or recurve cut closer to centre generally requires arrows of the same spine or slightly stiffer than the actual draw weight of the bow at your draw length. You may have to experiment to find the perfect spine to suit the combination of the bow and your technique. Number all your test arrows and record how they perform in a shooting test (this is known as 'clocking'); save the one which comes out best –this can be measured on the spine tester to provide a record of the spine you require.

Spining graph

The graph opposite indicates the degree of flexion required in a shaft for a particular bow weight, based on the AMO system; this is 'rule of thumb' stuff for the reasons described above. Some cultures don't have this 'scientific' approach, instead their fletchers and archers learn to assess the suitability and spine of an arrow by flexing the shaft, a technique needing some experience and skill. By and large the graph relates to the conventional western loose using a recurve bow; shooting with a thumb ring or off the 'wrong' side of the bow will modify the paradox and so affect choice of spine, Happy experimenting!

THE EFFECTS OF INCORRECT SPINE

The following advice is set out for right-handed archers, left-handers please *vice versa.*

An arrow that is too stiff will fly left, a whippy one to the right. It may strike the bow as it leaves and will fly erratically because it fails to bend around the bow correctly. Little can be done to major offenders if the arrows are too stiff –you could scrape some wood off the shaft to 'limber' it up a little, but it is best to make another set from lower spined shafts. An arrow which is too long for the archer's drawlength will act in a more

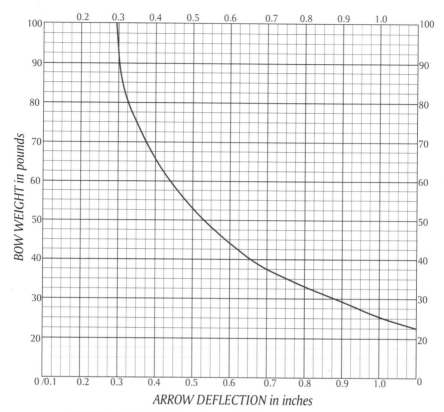

ARROW DEFLECTION in inches

SPINING GRAPH: Starting guide based on a recurve.
Spine for bows shooting around the handle may need to be reduced

whippy fashion, and is most likely to strike to bow in passing; it is also an inefficient use of the bow's stored energy as it will be shifting more weight than is needed.

Visual checks
Check all your arrows for tell-tale marks on the shaft indicating that they are consistently striking the bow in the same place: this generally means that your style has settled down, but your arrows are wrong.

Minor adjustments
Use a lighter pile to make it act more stiffly, a heavier one to add a little more flexibility. Check your arrowlength, particularly if the arrow strikes the bow as it leaves. The back of the pile should just touch your knuckle or the arrow shelf at full draw. There is a theory that adding more coats of finish will stiffen a shaft, but I've tried this using standard finishes and found it makes no appreciable difference.

THE SPINETESTER

There is only one way you can be absolutely sure of the spine rating of your arrowshafts: you need to beg, buy, borrow or (preferably) make yourself a spinetester. If you have several bows, like shooting different styles or just like experimenting, this is a vital piece of kit.

Making a spinetester

There are several types you can make yourself, and some designs are more simple than others. The design I have described here is fairly sophisticated, but it is easily made for very little expense from readily available materials, and will give you many years of accurate service.

You will need a micrometer to help with marking the gauge board.

A Baseboard: 18mm ply or MDF

B Arrow supports: make both adjustable for measuring shafts between 22 to 32 inches; (I slotted these over bolts in the baseboard and used wingnuts as shown) mark the base both sides to ensure the arrow pin reads accurately at the centre of the shaft.

C Rotating arrow supports (e.g.castors with groove cut around).

D Adjustable hinged support with...**E** a tilting screw to allow for zero-ing the pointer. (I used a nut inserted in the upstand with the bolt modified to be more comfortable on the thumb).

F Pivot point for pointer mechanism. This can be a simple metal pin bearing.

G 'Arrow pin' to rest on centre point of shaft.

H Counterweight to balance pointer so that it puts virtually no weight on the shaft.

J Pointer (you could use an old arrow shaft).

K Gauge board: cut 12x22 inch ply sheet and fix this temporarily while marking out then cut to shape. Mark in gradations of .025" using a micrometer under the arrow pin at G, over a range of 0" to 1.0". (I recommend you do this several times before making the markings permanent, just to be sure).

L 2lb weight applied to the mid-point of the arrowshaft: make up a lead weight, or cut the handle from a 2lb lump hammer and screw a cup hook into the wood remaining in the socket.

OTHER FACTORS AFFECTING SPINE

Arrow spine is not only a function of the shaft material's inherent flexibility, it is also affected by:

– arrow length: a longer arrow behaves more flexibly

– location of centre of balance/shape of the arrow e.g. a barrelled arrow will act more stiffly than a parallel one (see information on barrelled and bobtailed arrows, later).

An arrow's behaviour in flight can also be modified by altering the fletching size, shape and configuration. More of that later.

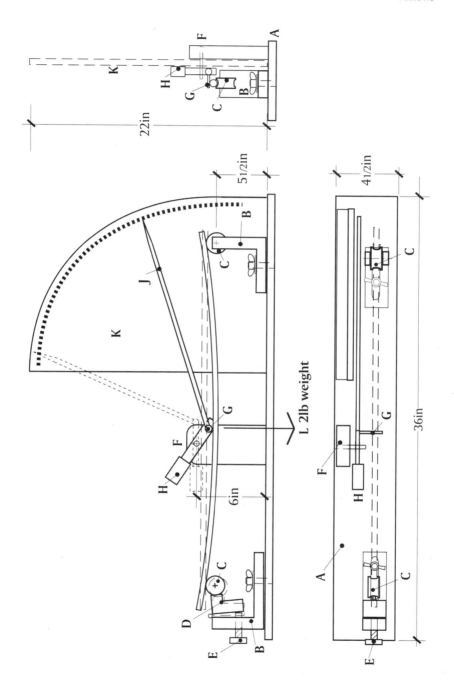

L 2lb weight

22in

5 1/2in

4 1/2in

36in

6in

29

The above guidance assumes that we are talking about target or field shooting, but if you shoot over longer distances at 'clout', roving marks or in flight competitions, a stiffer spine may be more suitable. You could also try using a lighter pile to reduce overall weight, reducing the fletchings or shaping the stele –trial and error is the principle here. There is information on making a flight arrow later in this chapter.

ARROW WEIGHT
The spine and weight of a shaft act together to influence the way an arrow flies, and while a set of arrows may have the same spine they will absorb the bow's energy differently according to their physical mass –it isn't just a case of heavier arrows not flying as far. Ideally your arrows should all be the same weight (preferably within 10 grains) in order to fly consistently. This is best achieved by weighing the shafts before you make up the arrows; while you could adjust weight by scraping a moderate amount of material from the shaft, this can affect spine, so re-check each shaft after you have modified it. Changing the weight of pile to adjust the overall weight is not recommended as it can affect flexion (spine) of the arrow.

Units of weight
Some traditionalists weigh their arrows in the 'old fashioned (Victorian) way', i.e. by weighing them against old coinage –hence the term "five shilling" or "the 2s.6d" arrow. Nowadays arrows are weighed in grains, and grain scales are available from good archery shops; you can also try powder scales from gun shops, but you must be sure that the scale weighs in the right range –a total arrow weight of well over 800 grains is not unknown, particularly with broadheads or bodkins at the business end. (800 grains=51.4 grammes, see 'Useful Data' for more details.)

FLETCHING
A traditional bow cries out for traditional fletchings, but unfortunately the true 'Grey Goosewing' of legend is hard to come by nowadays. If you find a source of good quality goose, turkey, or swan feathers, collect the pinions (these are the largest wing feathers) and save those with the best oil line –hold them up to the light and you will see a clear line which will indicate the limits of your final fletching shape.

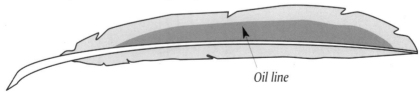

Oil line

Cutting feathers
Once you have selected the best pinion feathers and if necessary washed them in lukewarm water, cut the quill using a sharp knife, scalpel or razor

blade as shown. 'Cracking' the quill beforehand by hitting it along it's length with a small blunt object (e.g. knife handle) can help with cutting the feather vertically.

Stripping feathers

You can strip the feathers rather than cut them, this gives the fletching a 'snug' fit to the shaft. Stripping a feather needs skill or you can be left with a damaged quill; 'fresh' feathers are best as the ribs of long-stored feathers can be too dry and tough. If you do decide to strip them pull the feather away from the quill from the top down to the base using steady even pressure –practice makes perfect! This method also applies to commercial full-length feathers. If you cut the feather, keep it even in order to avoid separation of the barbs when they are glued to the shaft which can look untidy. I suggest you leave cutting to length until last, you will have more idea of the usable part once you have trimmed the rib.

The second cut reduces the rib on the side of the feather, and similar advice applies as for splitting the quill. You can thin the rib *before* you split the feather vertically if you find it easier to handle this way; whatever method you choose, a reasonable degree of dexterity is required!

Top'n'tail the feather to its optimum length.

Shaping

There are various ways of cutting the feather to your preferred shape.

The simplest method is with long scissors, using a template if necessary, this can also be done when the fletching is fixed on the shaft; if you have a shakey hand apply a strip of masking tape to the fletchings first. The more sophisticated fletcher can use a pre-shaped metal cutter, bashed with a hammer on a board! A feather burner is an excellent, if more technological, alternative. Before fixing the feather to the shaft, you may need to hold it in a clamp and file or sandpaper the base of the rib to ensure it lies flat and avoid the barbs separating.

31

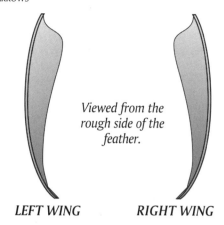

Viewed from the rough side of the feather.

LEFT WING   RIGHT WING

Feathers are either left wing or right wing depending on which side of the bird they are from. Arrows must have all of one type in order to maintain the stability and correct rotation of the shaft.

NOTE: A helical fletching jig must be the correct 'hand' to match the fletching. Jigs for angled fletching are usually adjustable.

A WORD (OR TWO) MORE ABOUT FEATHERS

Turkeys fly the ol' fashioned way, and do not have plastic rotors, so plastic vanes don't belong on traditional arrows. I would add:
- feathers are soft enough to reduce major flight difference and damage should they 'run the bow', or brush a tree or a leaf
- they are traditional
- they look good
- they even sound good!

The most easily available commercial fletchings are turkey, sometimes dyed, natural barred, or printed to simulate natural markings. Some of the dyes used can reduce the natural resistance to wear of some of the larger fletchings. Trial and error again, here.

Dyeing feathers

If you have obtained white turkey feathers and decide to dye your own, do this after you have stripped and washed them. I don't recommend you use cleaning chemicals as a preparation before dying as these will strip the oils and weaken the feathers. You can decide yourself whether to dye them before or after you've cut them to shape; I would recommend you use a cold dye, as boiling feathers for any length of time will destroy their oils and they can look a bit like they've been salvaged from a road kill. After dying, rinse the feathers in plenty of cold water, separate and straighten and lay them out to dry, preferably on towels.

WATERPROOFING

The main disadvantage of fletchings is their propensity to lie flat against the shaft at first signs of rain (and who can blame them?). This can be overcome by spraying them with silicon or wax based fabric waterproofer which is lightweight, but thorough. Don't overdo it, though!

SHAPE AND SIZE OF FLETCH
It's not just what it looks like, it's how it performs.
A large fletching will look nice, sound nice, be more 'forgiving' of a bad loose and fly more slowly than a smaller one. A large fletching will help straighten an arrow earlier in it's flight (very helpful if you possess a lousy loose); you will be reducing cast but in my view this doesn't matter over shots under 40 yards. Basically, it's the area of a fletching that matters, rather than it's shape, although trailing 'tails' will slow the shaft down a bit more.

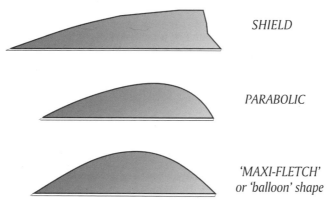

SHIELD

PARABOLIC

'MAXI-FLETCH'
or 'balloon' shape

SOME COMMERCIALLY AVAILABLE FLETCHING SHAPES

A TWIST IN THE TAIL
All arrows spin when they fly as the air passes differently over the smooth and rough sides of the fletchings; this spin increases if they are put onto the shaft at a slight angle (see the 'makings' section later). Spinning of the shaft helps straighten the arrow after the 'paradox' and stabilises flight. Further stabilisation is achieved by using helical fletching.

Helical fletching
Originally used to steady hunting shafts with large heavy broadheads at the business end, this means twisting the fletching around the shaft to increase speed of arrow spin and so straighten the shaft more effectively. Fletching jigs are available with left-hand and right-hand clamps to accommodate helical fletching. Advantages claimed for using 'helicals' can cause heated debate, so I can only express my o-pinion (sorry, pun intended): while a helical fletch slows the arrow down, I've found that this isn't significant over the average field course with shorter distances than those in target or clout shooting; the distance lost is outweighed by the improvement in flight, particularly if the archer's loose can be a little variable. After all, an arrow will also slow down if it's flailing around, so straightening it up early must be an advantage!

*For all fletching, the rough side of the feather should always
'face' into the wind.*

ANGLED FLETCHING

*The cock feather must be at
right angles to the nock.*

Fletching 'twists' around the shaft (Left wing shown).

HELICAL FLETCHING

WEAR AND TEAR

Whatever style and shape of fletching you use, you may notice wear on one particular feather on every arrow, this is usually caused by it touching ('running') the bow as it spins past. Adjustment of your bracing height could be the answer, or try using lower profile fletchings, lengthened in order to maintain adequate fletching area. As a last resort this problem can be cured by realigning the fletchings in relation to the nock, although most modern jigs don't accommodate this.

Reshape battered fletchings by steaming them over a pan of water, they will soon spring back into shape, however be careful not to overheat plastic nocks as they melt!

HORSES/ARROWS FOR COURSES

Target competitions

Targets range from 40 yards to 100 metres (depending on the type of round); between 90 and 144 arrows are shot in a round, so bows of lighter draw weight are usually preferred with lightweight, low fletched arrows. For longer target distances 3 inch parabolic or shield fletchings are usual; the arrows must be perfectly matched to each other and to the bow for consistency and accuracy. A heavy draw weight bow (say, 60lb plus) with a good cast can carry arrows with a larger fletching –it's your choice and don't be put off by any remarks implying that you are shooting real turkeys.

NOTE: please don't use broadheads at any target unless invited to do so. Usually bullet or lightweight piles are used for target shoots, as these do the least damage to traditional straw bosses. There is also resistance to allowing the heavier bows for safety reasons: ask the shoot organiser if you have any doubts.

Field archery

Most targets are within 40 yards on field courses, so accuracy rather than cast is the priority. A general guide is to use 4 inch fletchings for arrows up to up to 28 inches in length, and 5 inch or over for longer shafts. If you are really keen traditionalist, you may well choose to shoot 6 inch-fletched arrows out of a 90lb longbow, after all, large fletchings make a *lovely* sound as they fly! (But be prepared for some negative comments, and ask a shoot organiser about safety –some dislike the really heavy bows, and as they are putting in the work, it is only courteous to ask them if it's okay to shoot a 100lb-er). Long-nosed field piles are designed to reduce penetration into innocent woodwork. Of course, this isn't always effective, and a sturdy knife is still required at times to gouge the 'business end' from some tree which stepped in front of your arrow at an inopportune moment.

Clout shooting

At British Long-Bow Society clout meetings archers shoot 180 yards for men and 120 yards for women. Lighter bows obviously need help over these distances and forms of flight arrow are often used, having very small fletchings and modified shafts.

Roving marks

This is an historic form of long-range practice, shooting at various unmarked long distances, at 'marks (vertical stakes) usually between 100 and 300 yards away. Archers usually carry numerous arrows with various sized fletchings, weights of head etc. to cater for the different distances. I think the main thing is to have them brightly coloured in order to be clearly seen, not only by yourself, but by the hoards of careless wellies intent on stamping out the competition.

Roving/hoyle shooting

A traditional form of archery training, where natural features such as a tree stumps, molehills or tufts of grass are used as the mark (these are the 'hoyles'). These marks are usually at shorter distances than roving marks –up to 100 yards. The archer whose arrow lies nearest the mark gains the 'upshot' and nominates the next one. Blunts, 'judo' points and flu-flus are recommended for this.

'Standard' Arrows

Flight competitions for these are held under the rules of the British Long-Bow Society. These arrows are intended to simulate the heavy war or 'sheaf' arrow which was issued to longbowmen in the Middle Ages (a sheaf is 24 arrows); competitions for a 'Standard Arrow' took place in 1521, together with contests for 'bearing' arrows (specification unknown) and 'flight' arrows. Standard Arrows are usually fitted with a small broadhead (e.g. London Museum Type 16) or bodkin, fitted to a sturdy shaft. (See 'Useful Data' for specification).

ARROWMAKING MATERIALS

Shafts

Spining of shafts has already been covered earlier in this chapter: shaft diameters are generally 5/16in. or 11/32in. (occasionally 23/64in. and 3/8 in.) Port Orford Cedar has been the favoured arrow wood for many years, however recent availability and quality problems has forced a search for alternatives, particularly in the UK. 3/8in. shafts are available in dense woods (e.g. Ash) for heavy draw weight bows, 'war' and Standard Arrows.

Fletchings

Feathers must be all left wing or right wing on a shaft. Helical clamps must be left hand or right hand to suit. The rough side of the fletching should 'face' into the wind to assist arrow rotation which straightens it. I recommend you pick bright colours to start with, to help with finding the odd stray.

Nocks

Plastic nocks can be bought in a wide variety of colours and sizes and manufacturers adopt different shapes, some more substantial than others. Some nocks have a sharp 'nib' on the inside which can damage the string underneath the serving, particularly if they are too tight a fit and you won't notice this until it's too late. Check all your arrow nocks for string fit as described earlier. (See also 'self' nocks later)

Piles

These are available in various sizes, weights and shapes. Some are offered with sockets for 'tapered' or 'parallel' fit, according to how you prepare the

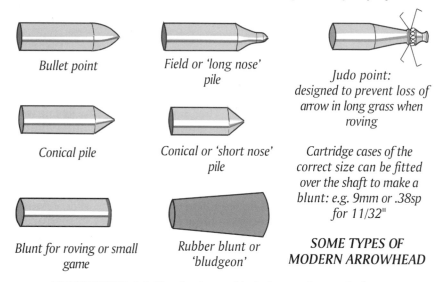

Bullet point

Field or 'long nose' pile

Judo point: designed to prevent loss of arrow in long grass when roving

Conical pile

Conical or 'short nose' pile

Cartridge cases of the correct size can be fitted over the shaft to make a blunt: e.g. 9mm or .38sp for 11/32"

Blunt for roving or small game

Rubber blunt or 'bludgeon'

SOME TYPES OF MODERN ARROWHEAD

PLEASE NOTE: it is illegal to hunt with the bow and arrow in the UK

shaft to receive the pile. Piles are available made from steel or brass, and are usually weighed in grains, the most common types being 100 or 125 grains, although some smaller styles are lighter. Diameters vary to suit available shaft sizes, most types being 5/16 or 11/32inch, other diameters (e.g.1/4inch) are available in limited shapes. Blunts, rubber bludgeons 'judo' points, whistlers and special lightweight flight piles are also available. Standard piles can be ground down to make blunts or remove weight, if the material is not too thin.

MAKING ARROWS WITH TAPERED PILES

The following recipe is for making a dozen field-style arrows. I've added variations at the end of this chapter. With practice, you will probably devise your own preferred method.

INGREDIENTS

1 doz. shafts, spined and weighed.
1 doz. piles (tapered) to suit shaft diameter.
1 stick 'hot melt'. (There are several different kinds, make sure you have the right one for wood and metal, not too slow-setting)
1 doz. nocks.
3 doz. fletchings.
1 tube clear all-purpose adhesive/fletching cement (with fine nozzle).
Polyurethane or acrylic varnish or lacquer.
Permanent ink for naming and numbering.
Strong thread to bind front end of quill.

EQUIPMENT

1 fletching jig.
1 small saw.
1 nock & point taper tool – size to suit shaft diameter.
1 pair pliers (for holding pile while heating).
Steel wool or fine sandpaper.
Heat source: e.g. gas ring or blow torch.

Optional

Paints for cresting.
Wood stain.
Cresting jig.
Dipping tube.

METHOD

1. Choose which end of the shaft is to be the pile end by checking the direction and nature of the grain –grain which looks jagged near the surface of the shaft should point to the rear of the arrow as a precaution against nasty splinters entering your bow hand on the rare occasion that the arrow should break on the bow .

'Primitive' style: e.g. Native American.

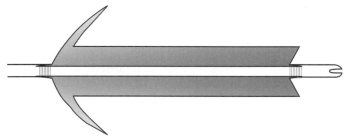

As above, with decoration. Notches in the feather and trailing tails were used.

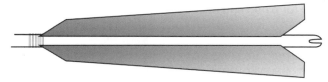

Another primitive shape, with the tails trimmed to prevent them touching the fingers, or face at full draw.

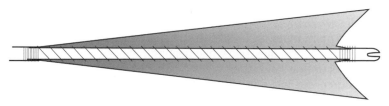

Medieval style, bound to the shaftment.

Another 'Medieval shape', but with helical twist.

SOME ALTERNATIVE FLETCHING SHAPES AND STYLES

2. Trim the shaft approx. 1 inch from the end, this is because the wood may have been damaged, lost its 'nature', or split at the end grain in storage.

3. Cut the pile taper using the tenon tool. Ensure that it is cut correctly aligned with the shaft, test fit the pile and adjust if necessary.

4. Clean out the inside of the pile with a 'cotton bud' (or similar) soaked in acetone, or other de-greasant. Cut some of the hot melt into small pieces and place some into the pile; heat the pile gently over a flame (holding with pliers unless your fingers are made of asbestos) until the hot melt is liquid but not too hot.

5. Insert the tapered shaft, rotating it to ensure that the hot melt is evenly spread. Press the shaft into the pile, ensuring it is aligned by frequent checking/spinning on the hand. I keep an egg cup of water nearby to cool the pile when it is on straight, and to reduce that burning sensation! The correct grade of hot melt will stay flexible enough to allow adjustment for several seconds. Any excess hot melt which squeezes out can be trimmed later. (If the pile tries to 'pop off' the shaft before the melt has set, you can relieve the trapped air by cutting a groove in the taper at stage 2.)

6. Cut the shaft to length. Draw length is generally measured from the bottom of the nock to the back of the pile.

7. Cut the nock taper with the tenon tool, again ensuring alignment.

8. If you wish to **stain** the shaft, or crown dip it, you should do it now

9. Fit the nock so that the string is across the grain – apply adhesive to the shaft, apply the nock, rotating it to ensure even spreading of glue.

   (Some people apply a varnish at this stage. I prefer to do this last as
   the varnish assists the adherence of the fletchings to the shaft.)

10. Fletching: carry out a dry run, inserting the fletching into the clamp, locate the feather against the shaft so that there is a distance of 1/2 to 1 inch approx. from base of the slot in the nock to the end of the fletch (you could mark the clamp accordingly to help with consistency). Place the fletching in the clamp, apply the adhesive thinly and evenly* to the quill and carefully locate the clamp onto the shaft. Glue drying times vary, but modern solvent-based adhesives are fairly quick, so you can usually do all fletchings in one 'sitting' and a cup of tea or two!

*Note: too much adhesive is as bad as too little for causing lack of adhesion, it is also unsightly.

11. Binding: if you don't want the painful possibility of a sharp quill entering your bowhand, it is recommended that you bind the front end of the rib with strong thread. This also helps prevent the fletching from lifting if the arrow passes through a leaky target, or tries to bury itself underground. Archers shooting off a shelf or rest can make do with adding an extra blob of glue to the quill, but I recommend the binding. You may need to trim the front end of the fletching against the shaft with a scalpel or very sharp knife in order to accommodate this.

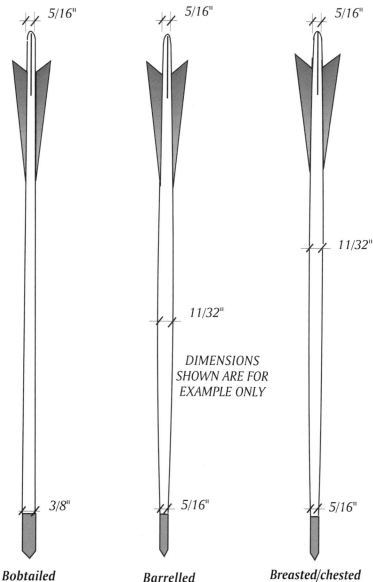

5/16"

5/16"

5/16"

11/32"

11/32"

*DIMENSIONS
SHOWN ARE FOR
EXAMPLE ONLY*

3/8"

5/16"

5/16"

Bobtailed
*The shaft is reduced
in diameter
towards the nock*

Barrelled
*These are reduced in
diameter at nock and
pile end*

Breasted/chested
*A variety of barrelled
arrow. The thickest part
of the shaft is toward the
nock end*

DIFFERENT SHAPES OF STELE

12. Cresting/marking: it is recommended (for some archery Societies it is required) that you name and number your arrows. I won't go into great detail, as the way you choose to do this is all part of personalising your arrows. Some people paint or 'crown dip' their arrows in a tube thus colouring the shaftment before fletching. Others crest them using a machine which rotates the arrow, allowing you to apply bands of paint evenly and quickly. There are good quality cresting jigs on the market, but you can make your own using a small motor obtained from a model shop; I've also heard of an electric screwdriver or an old cassette player being used; or rotate the arrow on a notched platform if you have a steady hand.

HANDY HINT: locate a clear band on your cresting, or mark your arrow at the place where the back of the bow should be when the arrow is nocked. This helps you to keep a constant check on bracing height while shooting, and warn you of bow problems or imminent string breakage before it is too late!

Finishing: apply your choice of varnish; I find three coats of polyurethane varnish is adequate, rubbed down with steel wool after each coat.

VARIATIONS IN ARROW MAKING
Parallel fit piles.
Some people prefer these to the taper-fit variety because they find them easier to align with the shaft, also some types of piles are not available for tapered fitting. The end of the shaft usually needs to be ground or filed to fit the pile over.

Two-part epoxy e.g. Araldite. (Piles only)
This is useful for people who have difficulty keeping their piles on –also some materials used for home-made butts can create friction-heat which causes hotmelted piles to come off. Heat can be used to remove the pile for repairs or shortening, although this is less easy than for a hot-melted pile. Note: some epoxies are brittle and inclined to break their bond if the arrow hits a hard object.

Pinning the pile.
For the same reasons as the above. A small hole is drilled into the side of the pile and a pin driven in to hold it on after it has been glued on.

'Superglue' (cyanoacrylate)
This can be used for nocks or fletchings if you are in a hurry –but there is little margin for error. If it gets damp during assembly it can turn white. You can also end up walking around with an arrow firmly glued to your fingers if you lose concentration.

BE A BIT DIFFERENT
If you love your workshop as much as you love shooting, then you may like to spend more time personalising your arrows in a number of ways, some of which are outlined below.

SELF NOCKS
Hardwood / horn inserts (tapered or parallel).

If you are going to make a fair number, you can fabricate a jig for these which slips over the shaft and acts as a saw guide. Correct grain direction is essential –i.e. inserts should be fitted parallel to the grain, in order that the nock can be cut across it. With the horn slip, taper the front of this so that you don't risk splitting the shaft. With self nocks, you must 'round' the inside of the slot in order to prevent undue string wear. Nock fit to string is also critical if you don't want to risk splitting the shaft or dry-loosing your bow.

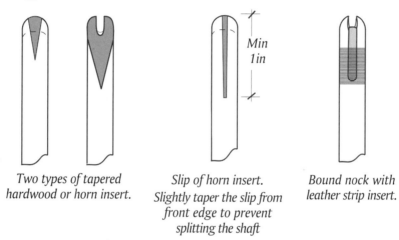

Two types of tapered hardwood or horn insert.

Slip of horn insert. Slightly taper the slip from front edge to prevent splitting the shaft

Bound nock with leather strip insert.

Min 1in

SOME STYLES OF SELF NOCK

Bound reinforcement.

This is most easily carried out when the whole fletching is bound to the shaft with strong thread in the traditional manner (see later); the binding can be carried on up the shaftment to help reinforce the nock, or to bind a leather insert which is slipped into the nock to cushion the string. Finish the binding by whipping the end and/or using Superglue to fix the loose end.

Test fit self nocks to the string and adjust with sandpaper and needle file as necessary: too loose a nock is better, if anything, as you can build up the serving: too tight and you can split the nock and put the bow at risk.

Coloured cock feathers.

Target archers generally use contrasting colours to differentiate the cock feather from the side feathers, and to personalise their arrows for easy recognition –however, it isn't strictly necessary as it doesn't take long to get used to nocking the arrow correctly. You can also mark or number the shaft at the cock feather.

Bound fletchings

When binding fletchings, keep the turns of thread fairly close, parallel and even (between four and six per inch is traditional) and ensure that the thread is pushed securely down at the quill, otherwise the fletching barbs will separate and look very untidy. Use strong (e.g. button) thread, but not too coarse, as this will also separate the barbs.

FITTING BROADHEADS

These must be fitted correctly aligned with the shaft to avoid erratic flight: there should also be adequate fletching to balance the broadhead and stop the shaft gadding. (See also section on helical fletching above). Fit the broadhead so that it is aligned with the string rather than perpendicular to it, this will assist aiming and prevent the larger barbed heads digging into the back of your bow. (They dig into your hand instead...)

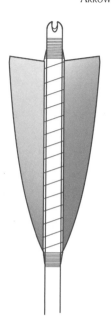

FOOTING

Bearing in mind the cost of shafts, and the fact that most arrows break behind the pile, you may wish to foot your arrows to reinforce the weak point. If you do this before making up the arrow, you can ensure that the arrows weigh the same and have the same centre of gravity –both characteristics are essential for a good set of matched arrows. Footing is also a handy method of saving arrows which have broken off behind the pile but which are otherwise perfectly serviceable. If you intend to foot many arrows, you can make a jig to taper the shaft, otherwise a good eye and a modelling plane will do the trick. Footings are also used to strengthen shafts which are barrelled down to small pile sizes (e.g. 1/4inch) and 'Judo' points where the risk of breakage behind the pile is greatly increased. Many people find footed shafts fly better because it modifies the centre of balance of the shaft.

A brief word on glues

Glue technology is improving all the time, and everyone has their favourite brand: make sure that the adhesives you use for self nocks and footings are fully waterproof, and not just water resistant (most readily available PVA based woodworking glues are not good enough). I recommend you try a good quality two-part epoxy resin which has suitable high strength, gap-filling properties and viscosity. (I've found some of faster drying varieties do not appear to be as strong as the slower setting ones.) If your wood surfaces fit perfectly, a powdered resin glue which is recommended for boatbuilding and other heavy duty uses is an excellent option. Proper measuring and mixing is essential.

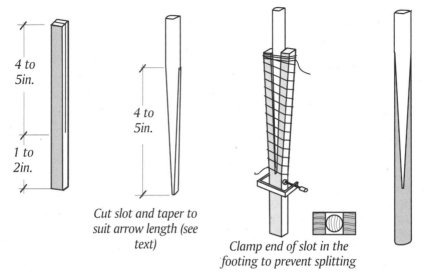

4 to 5in.

1 to 2in.

4 to 5in.

Cut slot and taper to suit arrow length (see text)

Clamp end of slot in the footing to prevent splitting

STEPS IN MAKING A SIMPLE FOOTED SHAFT

1. Use good quality offcuts from suitable hardwoods (e.g. greenheart, lemonwood, rosewood, black walnut) –your bowyer may supply them. Use a 3/8inch square section, and cut a slot as illustrated, across the grain to prevent splitting. The overall length of your footing depends on the finished length of the arrow; I suggest a total length of 6 inches. with a 4 inch. slot for most arrows, although you may wish to increase the footed length for arrows over 30inch. This will provide a 1/2 to 1 inch length of footing material behind the pile. These are guide dimensions, by the way, they are not set in stone!
2. Taper the shaft as illustrated, parallel to grain.
3. Temporarily reinforce the end of the footing slot with a clamp in order to prevent splitting.
4. Apply glue to both surfaces and insert the arrow into the footing, stopping 1/16inch short of the end of the slot.
5. Check alignment and bind string tightly around the footing.
6. Push the shaft home into the footing to ensure a tight fit.
7. When the glue is dry and the string is removed, plane excess wood from the footing, continually checking for alignment, the blade must be very sharp and set for fine work –a modellers plane works well.
8. Finish the footing using a hinged sanding block as illustrated in the 'Shafts' section.

FLU-FLUS

These arrows are designed to slow the arrow down rapidly, and are ideal for aerial shots or situations where you wish to reduce arrow speed, impact or penetration, e.g. while roving at hoyles or aerial shooting. In most cases they have a blunt fitted. A full length feather will be required.

1. Curl the feather by running the trimmed quill over an edge, similar to curling paper over a table edge, or strip the quill as described earlier to help the feather twist 'round the shaft.
2. Glue and pin one end of the feather about 6 inches from the base of the nock. (The curl of the feather will tell you which end to use).
3. Glue the base of the feather as usual, and twist it around the shaft, keep the turns approximately 1/2inch apart.
4. Glue and pin the last part of the rib in place.
5. When dry remove pins, bind the front of the quill as usual; carry on binding the feather to the shaft for its full length, whipping round the rib at the nock end.

An alternative method ('speed blunt')

This method produces a slightly faster arrow. Cut half a dozen 5 to 6 inch untrimmed fletchings from full length feathers: using a straight fletching jig, fix the first three fletchings in the normal way, then rotate the shaft 180 degrees in the nock locator and affix the other three. Bind the front end of the fletchings.

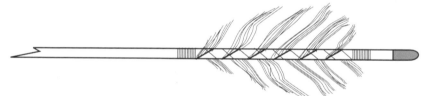

FLU FLU WITH 'WRAPPED ROUND' FLETCHING

ARROW CARE

If an arrow has hit a tree or other unfortunate object, always check it for damage (the arrow, not the tree) by flexing it while holding pile and nock, and for straightness by spinning it before replacing it in your quiver. If it is covered in mud (or worse) you may find a tassel handy; this is a woollen arrow cleaner suspended from the belt, otherwise you could use a bar towel or other absorbent cloth.

Bent arrows

These can be straightened by heating the shaft, either by friction from the hand or holding it over a low flame, and gently bending it back into alignment. If the shaft has 'chrysalled' or fretted (i.e. the wood fibres have creased along the bend) throw it away –not only is it useless, it is also dangerous to shoot it as it may shatter on the bow.

Damaged nocks

These can be replaced by carefully burning them off, you only need to catch them alight for a second or two, then push them off with a knife (warning: burning plastic sticks to the skin). The impecunious can use a microwave to remove fletchings and nocks from a broken (wooden only) shaft, but don't 'cook' the arrow remnants for more than a few seconds!

Battered fletchings

These can be revived by steaming them over a pan of boiling water.

ARROW STORAGE

Once you are home, store your arrows vertically in a rack made for the purpose, avoid keeping them in your quiver. A simple rack can be made by constructing a ply box fitted with two sheets of fine weldmesh, fix one layer 1 inch from the base and another at the top to ensure that the arrows are kept vertical. Arrows should be stored away from sources of direct heat.

FLIGHT ARROWS (BREASTED SHAFT)

The sight of a well-loosed arrow soaring into the air, with the fletchings flickering in the sunlight as they spin raises the traditional archers spirits like little else, particularly if it plummets towards the centre of a distant mark! A good flight arrow is special, it is also a fine compromise between various properties:

– a finely balanced shaft which will maximise 'glide'
– sufficient flexibility to clear the bow cleanly but stiff enough to straighten up almost immediately
– a fletching area large enough to provide adequate steerage, but as small as possible to minimise drag,
– as low a physical weight as possible but which has enough mass and strength to 'stand' in the bow: too light an arrow and you not only waste bow energy but also risk bow breakage, too heavy and it will not achieve the bow's potential
– a smooth surface with no steps, kinks etc. to disrupt the air flow.

Wonderful theories are put into practice with flight arrows: I recall one much-hyped set which had been designed by an aerodynamics specialist –they had a consistent but boomerang-style performance. Moral: allow plenty of room for safe flight testing. Don't be dismayed if you need to make many flight arrows to get that perfect one which flies far and true. (Try to record the statistics of this one before you break it!) The match of arrow to bow in this pursuit is critical, so time and space for experimentation is necessary: yes, you can buy flight arrows, but to get the maximum possible distance out of your particular bow with your individual shooting style, I strongly recommend you make your own, carrying out any fine adjustments necessary to achieve those extra all-important yards.

MAKING A FLIGHT ARROW

The following is based on a breasted arrow with a centre of balance just in front of centre, using a 5/16inch shaft reduced to 1/4inch at both ends, this is a reasonable start for a 60lb longbow or equivalent. Don't put your bow at risk by using too light an arrow –you are effectively dry-loosing it; (if your bow kicks badly in the hand on loosing it is a sign that you may be pushing your luck). Start within safe margins –you can always gradually reduce the arrow size and weight after test shooting.

MATERIALS

5/16inch best quality shaft

It is difficult to beat a good quality Port Orford Cedar shaft for weight to strength ratio if you can get one of good quality. Whatever you use, select a straight-grained shaft with close and parallel growth rings running from end to end. Use one spine grade above that you normally use: a barrelled or breasted arrow will generally act more stiffly than a parallel one but you will be removing quite a bit of the material in shaping it. For aerial shooting a stiff spine works well.

Footing material

Use close- and long-grained wood of good quality, e.g. wenge, bloodwood, purpleheart or black walnut – all are excellent for footing flight shafts.

1/4inch pile

Try 25 grains to start: too light a pile and the arrow can fly badly left (for a right hander).

1/4inch plastic nock

Use a substantial nock for the heavier bows. (Fit to string is critical).

Fletchings:

I suggest you start with 1 1/2inch parabolic which can be cut down later.

METHOD

1. Foot the shaft to reinforce it just behind the pile –a simple two-splice footing as described elsewhere in this chapter will be fine –too many splices will be weak point, particularly if used on a small diameter shaft (I would suggest three splices maximum); this footing can be shorter than the conventional target footing to keep the overall weight down, but as you will be reducing the diameter of the shaft a reinforced length of about 1/2inch behind the pile is recommended.

2. Round the footing with a sharp plane: continually check that the footing is aligned correctly.

3. Mark the midpoint of the shaft and the centre of balance (COB) which at this juncture will be quite far forward; once the pile is fitted it will move even further forward, so more material will need to be removed from the head end than the shaftment. Measure and mark all round the shaft as illustrated; this will make it easy to remove material evenly; you can also apply a light stain to help visually.

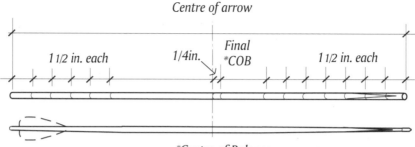

Centre of arrow

*Final
COB

1 1/2 in. each   1/4in.   1 1/2 in. each

Centre of Balance

MARKING THE SHAFT FOR BREASTING

4. Reduce the shaft: use the finest setting on your plane with a sharp blade (a modellers plane fitted with a razor blade works well); gently remove material from all around the shaft, starting at the first mark; replace the removed mark and plane back to the next and so on, until a taper is achieved, with a diameter at both ends which is just too large to fit the pile and nock. Check the shaft regularly for straightness and roundness throughout.

5. Sand the shaft with fine grit paper, using a block as described earlier in this chapter. Temporarily push on the pile and glue the nock.

6. Re-check the COB and adjust it's location to about 1/8 to 1/4 inch in front of the midpoint: remove more material from the pile end, making sure that you don't remove too much, causing a waist behind the pile –we are looking for sm-o-o-o-o-oth, here! If your plane is a bit too drastic for fine tuning, use a fine scraper such as a sharp knife or blade, marking round the shaft as necessary. Sand gently, this is surgical work! Once you are happy with the COB, sand the shaft smooth ensuring joints etc. are even with no steps etc. It is easier to varnish the arrow at this point, then straighten and polish it smooth before applying the fletchings.

7 Apply fletching: a three fletch applied straight will be plenty to start with. You could experiment with moving them up the shaft, but usually the farther back on the shaft they are the better steerage you will get. If you feel you have overfletched the arrows cut them down (take some scissors with you when test shooting!)

SOME NOTES ON FLIGHT SHOOTING

Leonardo da Vinci used flight shooting to describe how movement effects impetus, describing that if everything is moving forward at the point of release, additional energy is imparted to the arrow: you will see archers run, leap, throw their bow arms forward –even yell to try and get that extra yard or two. However, this isn't much point without control: at the time of loosing your bow should be at the optimum angle (45 degrees or just under) the loose must be fast –a slashing loose is good technique, and the release clean. Assuming the brace height, nocking point etc. is all correct, you will see that arrow really go! Then you'll be back in the workshop…

"If I just move the centre of balance back a little and reduce the fletchings, maybe go up a spine…"

QUIVERS: A SIDE NOTE
Traditional archers generally need to carry around more arrows than their high-tech counterparts, particularly if out roving. The size of arrowheads (bludgeons, judo points, broadheads etc.) together with the wide variety of types needed to enjoy all aspects of traditional archery, mean that a capacious quiver is essential, whether it is of the side or back variety. Generally speaking for most traditionalists a holster type is woefully inadequate.

Side or back quiver?
This is a matter of personal preference as both types have advantages and disadvantages: if you want to carry around a large number of different types of arrow, you may find it easier to select a particular arrow from a side quiver; back quivers are easier when negotiating difficult ground. If you elect to use a side quiver and are going to be shooting over rough terrain, I'd recommend one which hangs vertically from the belt –angled ones can tip and unship the arrows under your feet if you're not careful. I've known archers who have had a special all-purpose quiver made which can be adjusted to hang from a belt or used as a back quiver. Many seasoned traditional archers have personalised quivers, made to their own specification and incorporating pouches for their archery survival kit: spare strings, wax, hip flasks etc.

6. STRINGS

Strings are often much neglected and taken for granted by archers –until they break, that is! Always carry a spare string around with you when shooting, preferably one that is shot in and has a correct nocking point. For bow preservation, be prepared to replace the string at first signs of wear; I suggest you replace a Dacron string after 2,000/2,500 shots, and a hemp or linen string after 1,000 shots at the very most.

STRING MATERIALS

There seems to be a constant search for faster strings, using modern materials which have less mass in relation to strength, but be warned, not all modern materials are suitable for traditional bows.

1. Dacron.

This is the most popular, and cheapest material for bowstrings. It is available in different strengths in order to reduce the number of strands and so reduce the weight of the string. A lighter string will be faster but more 'critical' to shoot than a heavier one.

2. Kevlar, Dyneema, Fast flight etc.

Do not use these string materials on any traditional bow unless the bowyer has approved them. These materials have little stretch, and therefore can 'shock' the limbs of a bow sufficiently to break them. I don't feel it's worth risking the bow however much cast is improved.

3. Hemp.

This is for the real traditionalist; the very best hemp produces a fine, forgiving string, but will have a limited life when compared with Dacron. Hemp has excellent natural water resistance. Anything other than the finest quality hemp yarn produces a 'lumpen' or weak string.

4. Linen (Flax).

Characteristics for linen yarn are similar to hemp. Fine unbleached Irish linen thread produces strings which are comparable to Dacron in thickness to strength ratio; these have excellent shooting qualities but generally wear more rapidly.

Other string materials

If you have made your own bow, particularly if it is a 'primitive' design, you may like to experiment with other string materials such as silk, nettle (or other vegetable) fibres and sinew (the latter stretches in moist atmospheres). Many of these raw materials are short in length and when being made up into a string, the ends must be overlapped and corded evenly and strongly into the whole, so I recommend plenty of practice at this before you test such a string in your bow; pre-stretching corded strings by hanging them up with weights tied to them for a time can also help. It is a good idea to test the string to ensure it can take least 4 times the draw weight of your bow before using it as a broken string can mean a broken bow.

Breaking strain

To assess breaking strain of potential string material, secure a strand to your bowscale and pull; if the thread (or string) is particularly strong, use pulleys etc. as necessary –your wall tiller may be useful here. Secure your scale very firmly as some materials may be stronger than you think! Record the poundage at which the material breaks several times and take the average reading –it is wise to be conservative at this point! Fix the string or yarn using rounded and padded surfaces, as sharp or rough edges can cause failure before you reach the true breaking strain.

TYPES OF STRING

The 'endless' string.

This is the type of string most commonly found on recurved bows; it is constructed by winding the thread continuously in a loop to form the main body of the string, a section at each end is then served together to form the loops for the nocks.

The Flemish string.

This is made up of separate strands cut to length and made up into two or more plies; the top loop is formed by 'laying in' the end of the plies with the main body of the string, using a rope-twist cording method. (Instructions are contained later in this chapter). The 'laid-in' loop is stronger than the single served loop of the endless string because all the strands are used rather than half the number. There are two ways of forming the loop for the lower nock of a Flemish string:

TIMBER, or BOWYER'S HITCH
Adjustable knot for the lower loop of a traditional Flemish string.

The timber hitch

Many longbow traditionalists use a string with one loop for the top nock, and a corded length for the lower nock which can easily be adjusted by use of the 'bowyer's hitch' (or 'timber hitch').

Double looped strings

The top loop is generally larger to ease removal from the upper nock on unstringing.

It is a matter of preference which type of string you use, and there is no hard and fast rule. There are advantages and disadvantages to both.

Using a hitch

The Flemish string with bowyer's hitch is maintained by many to be traditional and the best for the English longbow, being the most easily adjustable. I believe the hitch was used historically because the strings were mass produced and a hitch allowed a 'one size fits all' sales policy. Unfortunately a timber hitch can slip, causing problems with bracing height, or it can slip to one side, twisting the lower limb. Some string materials have been given an 'oily' rather than waxy protection by the manufacturers and do not hold a hitch well, so apply copious amounts of proper beeswax in this instance. The kink in the string at the hitch can be a weak point, particularly as this is the end which gets dipped in soily substances (and worse) –additional waxing is a help with this, too.

The two-loop string

For bow preservation, I prefer the double-looped 'Flemish' string; fine tuning of the bracing height is achieved by adjusting the number of twists in the string which means that it should be made close to the correct length in the first place. Save an old complete string as a basic measure for making the new.

HOW MANY STRANDS?

Strings must have a minimum strength of 4 times the bow draw weight in order to be safe. Allowing for normal wear and tear, and the need to have a string thick enough to fit the nock, at least 10 strands of Dacron B50 is recommended for the traditionalist, even for the lighter bows.

Assuming Dacron B50 is used, the following is a guide to recommended strands for a Flemish string:

Bow weight	No.
20 - 30lbs	10
30 - 45lbs	12
45 - 60lbs	14
60 - 80lbs	16
80 - 100lbs	18
Over 100 lb	20

For flight strings you may wish to omit a strand or two, but double check the string and replace it more often if you shoot a lot of arrows.

HOW TO MAKE A SIMPLE STRING

The next few pages attempt to describe in simple stages a method of making a two-loop Flemish string; use of a board as described avoids the bird's nest which can occur with some string materials which –when combined with novice thumbs– can cause severe aggravation at a time when you just want to string that bow and get on with shooting it! A hook in the wall will work perfectly well, but I've found using the board can ensure even tension and is useful if you make many strings of different lengths; it also helps if you need to unravel a string to lengthen or shorten it, or adjust loop size if necessary.

Two ply or three ply?

I've used two plies for simplicity in the following description; a 3-ply string will be smoother and can be faster –the principles for making this are exactly the same. It's essential that all strands are in equal tension in order to maintain the full strength of the whole.

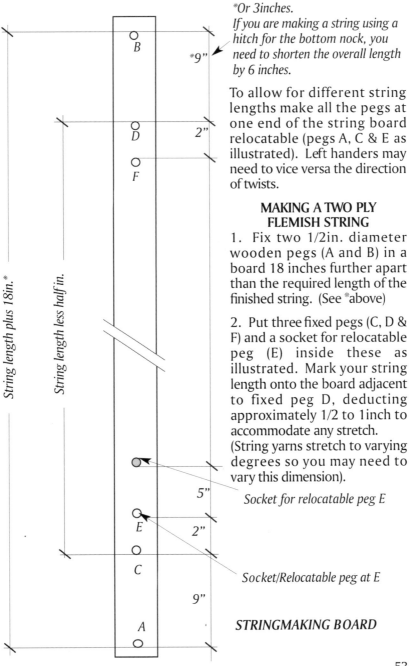

B

*9"

D 2"

F

*Or 3inches.
If you are making a string using a hitch for the bottom nock, you need to shorten the overall length by 6 inches.

To allow for different string lengths make all the pegs at one end of the string board relocatable (pegs A, C & E as illustrated). Left handers may need to vice versa the direction of twists.

MAKING A TWO PLY FLEMISH STRING

1. Fix two 1/2in. diameter wooden pegs (A and B) in a board 18 inches further apart than the required length of the finished string. (See *above)

2. Put three fixed pegs (C, D & F) and a socket for relocatable peg (E) inside these as illustrated. Mark your string length onto the board adjacent to fixed peg D, deducting approximately 1/2 to 1inch to accommodate any stretch. (String yarns stretch to varying degrees so you may need to vary this dimension).

5" *Socket for relocatable peg E*

String length plus 18in. *

String length less half in.

2"

E

C

9"

A

Socket/Relocatable peg at E

STRINGMAKING BOARD

53

3. Loop your string material around the outermost pegs until you have sufficient strands. (See earlier in this chapter for recommended number)

4. After lightly waxing the strands to stop them separating, cut the strands adjacent to peg A.

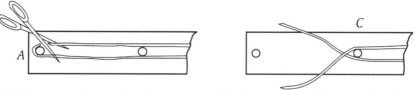

5. Using peg C, cross the plies over, and begin roping as illustrated below to form the cordage for the top loop. The number of turns depends on the size of the limb which it has to slide over and the size of nock: between 12 and 16 is about right (the lower loop is usually a little smaller –see also note below). Wax this corded length well.

FORMING THE LOOP Stage 1: turn the strand clockwise between finger & thumb while crossing it anti-clockwise over the other. Repeat, thus forming corded length for loop.

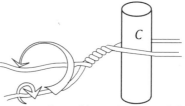

6. Carefully remove the corded part from peg C, and loop it around the inner peg E (this is because the string shortens as you twist it). Cross the ends of the plies over and wax each one together with the corresponding main ply of the string. (See following illustration)

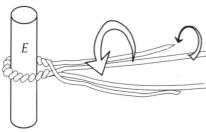

FORMING THE LOOP Stage 2: thoroughly wax the ply ends together with the main plies, twist & cross the plies as before.

7. 'Lay-in' the ends with the main body of the string by roping the plies together as described in stage 5, thus forming the top loop, until the ply ends run out (stagger these in order to taper the splice neatly into the main body of the string). Wax well.

Note: ensure the loop sizes are correct for your nocks: not too tight, for easy stringing, and not too large which may cause twisted limbs or de-stringing.

8. Carefully remove the other end of the string from peg B, and relocate your laid-in loop from peg E to C. Untwist the two plies from each other. Relocate peg E to the inner socket (this peg will keep the two plies separate and stop the top loop unravelling while you form the second).

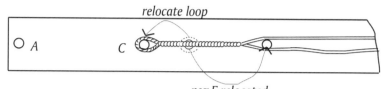

9. Pull the plies taut to ensure that all threads are in equal tension and wax lightly. Then cut the two plies at the other end of the board.

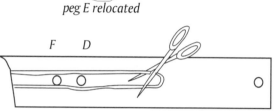

(If you wish to use a bowyer's knot, just cord the last 4-6in. of the string and tie a knot. It may be worth serving this end, because the kink formed by the hitch is the weakest part of the whole string).

10. Counter-twist each of the plies clockwise, rolling them between your finger and thumb (the number of turns is a matter of trial and error, I 'roll' each ply 35-40 times). These are needed to counter the twists made in forming the next loop.

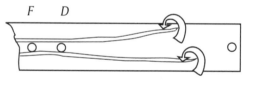

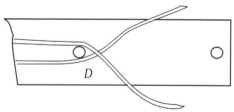

11. Wax the last 12 inches of the two plies, cross them around peg D, ensuring both plies are in equal tension and cord the lower loop as you did the first; a smaller loop is usual for the lower nock.

12. As you twist the string it will shorten, so relocate the loop to peg F and 'lay in' the second loop into the main skeins as before.

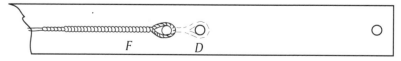

13. Carefully remove the second loop from peg A, and counter twist the string a few turns anti-clockwise to prevent the splice unravelling, before removing the first loop from peg F and doing the same at this end (this assists in obtaining an smooth string). The final number of twists in the string depends on the adjustment of bracing height, there should be a minimum of one turn per inch, but not so many that the string twists back on itself.

14. As in culinary terms, wax well before serving

SERVING

The central serving is 'whipped' onto the string, a technique you may be familiar with, but I shall attempt to describe it all the same. I would recommend a soft serving thread (they can be bought in several colours and different thickness) or linen for the traditionalist, and a serving tool for speed and even tension; although a serving tool is not strictly necessary if you don't intend to make many strings, there is nothing more annoying than trying to find that little spool which has just leapt out of your butterfingers as you are in the middle of the task...and then having to rewind the thread before you can carry on.

1. Mark the area to be served on the string. (this is approx. 2inches above the proposed nocking point and 7in. below.

2. The serving should wind the same way as the string in order to maintain tension particularly if you are not using a serving tool. (Imagine a rolled tube of paper, and how you tighten the roll by turning it from the inside, and apply the same principle)

3. Double back a length of serving as Illustrated.

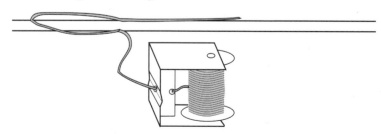

4. Commence serving for 10 turns.

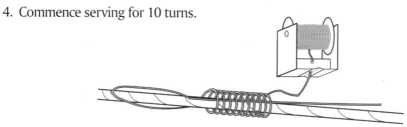

5. Pull the end of the thread through, then serve tightly over it with the serving tool for a few more turns. . .

. . . and trim loose end.

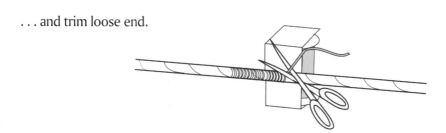

6. Continue serving until within 1/4inch of the end of the served length, maintaining constant tension. (Not too tight –the served part of the string should still be relatively flexible)

7. Cut the serving free of the spool, leaving a tail approximately 8 inches long (you can choose not to cut the serving material, but you will need to leave a large loop during the next step to accommodate the serving tool during the counter-turns).

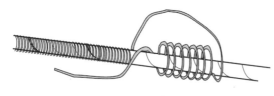

8. Turn the free end of the serving thread around the string for 10 to12 counter-turns as illustrated.

9. Continue serving over the free end, leaving a 'tail' sufficiently long to grasp and pull through when you have exhausted the counter-turns.

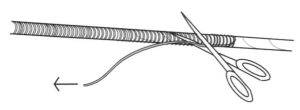

10. Pull the free end back through, and trim.

11. If you have doubts about the security of your serving, a drop of 'superglue' on the ends will not do any harm.

WAX LYRICAL

Wax your string regularly, but not the serving. Use a good quality pure beeswax. It is a good idea to remove the string from the bow occasionally and thoroughly wax the loops.

but. . .

Do not overwax –if the bowstring looks like a candle it will be slow. Just make sure that the wax has penetrated sufficiently into the string by rubbing vigorously with a piece of leather or thick paper, until the string and wax is heated by the friction. Remember to wax the loops as these can be major points of wear, particularly the bottom loop which comes into contact with mud and dirt most often. If your serving does become particularly sticky with wax, an application of French chalk (to the serving only) will help you maintain a reasonably friction-free loose.

NOCKING POINT

You should initially apply a temporary nocking point –narrow masking tape is a good start. Once your new string has been 'shot in' and will no longer stretch, apply a permanent nocking point. More information on nocking points is in chapter 4 on 'Tuning'.

7. CARE OF YOUR BOW

LONGBOWS (and other all-wood bows)

Correctly treated a good longbow will give you many years of service, and there are still some fine Victorian bows in use today. Bows do break occasionally and English longbows with their deep, stacked limb section can be particularly vulnerable. However, you can greatly improve the longevity of your bow by observing some basic common-sense guidelines regarding its care.

Some things that will break a bow

– allowing someone other than yourself to draw it up or shoot it
– holding for a long time at full draw (2 seconds should be more than enough for a longbow)
– overdrawing the bow beyond the designed draw length: NOTE: this can happen if you draw it up without an arrow on it, allow a stranger to draw it up, or have the bracing height far too high
– stringing your bow incorrectly or carelessly. (See illustrations later in this chapter for the recommended method)
– incorrect bracing height (far too low is as dangerous as too high)
– allowing a string to get so worn that it breaks
– dry-loosing the bow: this includes shooting aluminium or carbon arrows out of it, they are too light
– shooting a bow which is damaged, however minor you may think the flaw is
– 'string walking' i.e. changing your finger position on the string, thus inconsistently and unevenly loading the limbs
– having the arrow nocks are too tight on the string because this can cause wear under the serving where you won't notice it. Follow kaputt!!
– likewise, if the arrow nocks are too loose, you are effectively dry-loosing the bow
– failing to 'ease' the bow when it has not been shot for some time, particularly in very cold weather.

How to help preserve your longbow

– regularly check the bracing height, usually between 6 and 7 inches for the average longbow, you can mark your arrows to assist with this; it is particularly important if you are shooting in a new string
– maintain a consistent loose. (Preferably 'mediterranean' –one finger over, two fingers under the arrow nock)
– on unstringing the bow, check it for any damage, also after any unfortunate 'knock' while shooting
– unstring the bow to rest it if you are not shooting for a while ('self' yew bows in particular may lose cast on warm days)

– when stringing, ensure that pressure is kept even on both bow limbs, preferably by using a double looped stringer
– check that the string loops are located correctly in the nocks before drawing up, particularly if you use a bowyer's hitch
– regularly wax the string; change it if there are any signs of wear
– warm the limbs by rubbing them when shooting in freezing temperatures (particularly yew)
– if the bow has not been shot for some weeks, 'ease' the bow into a bend by flexing it repeatedly on stringing, do not pull immediately up to full draw.

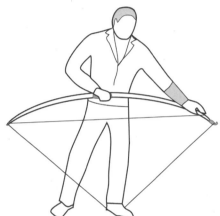

LEFT: My preferred method for stringing a bow, particularly the English longbow, using a cord stringer: this usually needs an additional notch for the stringer in the top bow nock as illustrated above. Ensure that your foot is on the middle of the stringer in order to load the limbs evenly.

RIGHT: An alternative method for stringing a longbow, although this can put extra stress on the lower limb if not carried out correctly.

STRINGING A BOW
For both methods even pressure and a thorough check that the string (and stringer) is correctly positioned in both nocks is essential.

STRINGING
The principles of stringing are simple –avoid putting undue, uneven pressure on the working part of the limbs, i.e. when stringing, restrict pressure to the nocks and the handle. Overstressing any single point on the limb (including the area close to the fadeouts on a recurve or AFB) is akin to breaking a stick over your knee. There are various other methods of

stringing, some mentioned in historic texts, including the 'step through' and even 'treading' the bow (you can guess what that means) –but they are potentially bow-threatening so I wouldn't recommend them if you want to preserve your bow in good condition.

A PLEA FOR SOME RESPECT. . .

Above all, whatever the weather and ground conditions, please don't use your bow as a prop, paddle, walking stick, arrow rake etc. This may sound obvious, but I have seen some awful things being done to (and with) a longbow!

MAINTENANCE (GENERAL)

You should regularly inspect your bow for signs of damage or wear, this is best done when drying/cleaning it after a shoot; in any case, always check your bow thoroughly after stringing it and before drawing it up. Apart from glue joint failure, other signs of damage to look out for are:

Scratches or breaches in the finish

There are many good finishes available nowadays so ask your bowyer about maintaining protection, cleaning etc. for the finish given your bow. You can check your bow for any signs of damage while cleaning and polishing it.

Lift in backing

'Lifting' of hickory backing

This is generally a fault in the wood, and usually occurs as a result of weakness in the hickory; this flaw can be exacerbated by misuse, or develop through plain 'old age'. In any event, if caught early enough it can be bound and strengthened or repaired in order to reduce the possibility of a broken bow.

Chrysals or frets

Chrysals (all-wood bows)

This fault occurs on the belly of a wood bow and is caused by the collapse of fibres under compression. It's not necessarily terminal, a top class bowyer may be able to scarf in a new piece of belly wood –the success of this repair depends on the style, age and quality of the bow.

Reasons for chrysals forming are many –they can result from misuse, a weakness in the material, uneven tiller, poor quality wood, old age or a combination of any or all of these!

'Bruising' of the back or belly (all-wood bows)

It is difficult to assess the degree to which this stops being cosmetic and becomes bow-threatening, although if it occurs in the major 'working' part of the bow (central section of limb) it is best to consult the bowyer as soon as possible for advice. Generally speaking any bruising of the belly is more hazardous than minor bruising of the back of the bow.

Twisting of a bow limb

This can occur on any bow through misuse, bad stringing practice, incorrect storage, or just plain old age. A bow will shoot perfectly well despite being twisted, providing the string is not too badly misaligned –it should lie within the handle when you squint down the bow; if you can feel the bow twist in the hand on drawing up and are not happy with the degree of twist, ask your bowyer for advice.

Incorrect tiller

This can occur if the bow is too-frequently rested on one of it's limbs (usually the lower) during or directly after shooting when unbraced, thus causing the limb to follow the string to a greater degree than the other. The bow may lose cast as a result; usually it can be re-tillered, perhaps with some loss of poundage.

TRANSPORTING THE BOW

It is recommended that you carry your longbow or flatbow in a cloth bag, not a waterproof one, and make sure that the bow is dry before you put it away. When travelling a long distance, or any time when extra protection is needed, some archers transport their longbow in a plastic pipe (e.g. a drain or soil pipe); a large diameter may be required to accommodate any permanent curvature in the limbs.

STORAGE

When you unstring the longbow after shooting, you may notice that the limbs retain a slight curve –this is known as 'following the string'. If the bow is correctly rested, this curvature should reduce; it is important to prevent a permanent 'set' developing in the bow, therefore avoid storing the bow by resting it on the lower nock, instead, hang it by a loop from the top nock, or (the best method for most bows) horizontally on a wall rack or pegs as illustrated below.

PREFERRED STORAGE METHOD   *support mid-limb*

CARE OF OTHER TRADITIONAL BOWS

Most of the criteria which I have already outlined for the care of longbows still apply when shooting any 'self' or wooden bow, whether flatbow, primitive or recurved. In addition:

Flatbows/Recurves with fibreglass

While these bows are more tolerant to abuse than longbows, care must still be taken in order to ensure their longevity and continued good performance.

– avoid lending them to archers with different (especially longer) draw lengths

– great care in stringing is required; use a 'saddle' or a 'double pocket' type stringer if possible; do not 'step through' a flatbow or recurve to string it as the depth of handle or riser can cause the bow to twist suddenly and violently, possibly resulting in damage to the limbs and/or breakage

–always check that the string is correctly located in the nocks before drawing up, this will avoid twisting the limbs, or even worse, a sudden 'unstringing' at full draw

– check that there are no sharp edges to the glassfibre which can cut the string at the nocks, or while sliding the string loop along the limb while bracing

– flatbows and recurves must always be unstrung when not in use

– it is wise to store these bows on a rack, out of the way, although it is not strictly necessary.

– avoid storing close to direct heat or in a hot car

– check the fibreglass laminations regularly for deep scratches, chips or splits, and consult your bowyer if necessary.

RUNNING REPAIRS

Your shooting kit should be well enough prepared for a day's shooting, but mishaps will happen! You may need to carry out running repairs while some distance away from your toxomobile, so it is a good idea to carry around material to repair the nocking point (tape or dental floss), a spare string which is shot in preferably with a correct nocking point and a small block of beeswax; a few spare nocks and suitably quick setting glue may not be a bad idea, either.

It has also been known for archers to carry around hot melt, spare piles, a box of matches, aspirin, insect repellent, whisky, gin, brandy and a spare longbow.

8. MAKING A 'PRIMITIVE' BOW

There is nothing in archery to equal making and shooting your own bow, including the knowledge that there is no other like it in the world! This chapter is intended to encourage all archers to try their hand at making a traditional bow. You will need a mixture of intuition, good sense, some small practical skill, a reasonable 'eye', and (in case of failure) perseverance and a sense of humour; if you shoot a 'primitive' bow you probably already have plenty of the latter!

Bowmaking is a vast subject; even something as simple as a 'primitive' bow has had many thousands of words devoted to it, practical, historical, technical and sometimes contentious. My view is that, while there are several basic sensible and practical guidelines for making a working bow, you should not be hidebound by dogma, or discouraged if you can't find (or afford) the perfect stave –if you have the enthusiasm and some basic skills –why not give it a try? Many a fine bow has been turned out of an unpromising stave because the right design for the wood's characteristics has been chosen and the bowyer has made a particularly good job of it. Good workmanship applied to what is considered to be second-rate bow wood can frequently produce a better bow than bad workmanship on a top quality stave.

The One Golden Rule

Don't be daunted by the idea that you must come up with the perfect bow first time. It is not essential to obtain visual perfection or get brilliant cast from your bow; look for character and individuality in the wood you are using and work with it. You will have made something unique that has a history going back thousands of years.

APPROACHES TO BOWMAKING

'Engineering' a stave

This isn't the approach I will be encouraging in this chapter, although it is an excellent way of turning out reliable quick-shooting bows: basically it means imposing a particular bow design on the wood, usually by gluing a number of laminations into a stave, thus reducing the risk of material failure; it also allows the bowmaker to use the relative properties of the materials to best advantage, so enhancing performance and longevity. Many English longbows and modern flatbows are made this way today.

Crafting a 'self' bow

This means working with the natural material to produce the best bow from a particular stave, taking into account it's unique characteristics. Most of the following bows I describe are of this type, and all primitive bows, in my view, should correspond to this principle. This applies to 'self' bows in the main part, but can also include bows which are backed after completion to aid their survival rather than enhance their performance.

WHAT IS A 'PRIMITIVE' BOW?

At it's most basic a primitive bow is a 'bent stick'. A self longbow, for instance, is a primitive design technically speaking. On the other hand, some bows made by so-named 'primitive' cultures are very advanced in design when considered with regard to the materials available to them. (See chapter 9 for information on making some of these bows). Purists insist that a truly primitive bow has to be made using exclusively primitive materials, tools and techniques. For some novice bowmakers this is asking a bit much, and my intention here is to encourage the beginner; if you become interested in using primitive hand tools and entirely natural materials, you will need to refer to more specialised references on primitive technology.

WHY START WITH A FLAT BOW?

I will start by explaining the basic principles of making a wooden bow, using a flatbow made from a board as an example; these principles are fundamental to all traditional bowmaking, and the beginner is more likely to succeed (and so gain confidence) by starting with a flat-limbed long bow rather a design which is more demanding of wood and craftsmanship, such as the stacked design of the traditional English longbow.
This is because:
  – you can make an effective wide-limbed bow out of a larger range of available woods
  – the bow is less likely to 'chrysal'(fret) because of the shallow limb section, i.e. the woodfibres of the belly are under less compressive stress than those of a deeper sectioned bow
  – a long-limbed bow is less likely to fracture
  – a bow with a large width to depth ratio is less likely to twist badly, and this is easy to spot and correct if it does
  – because there is less compression of the belly wood, string follow is reduced
  – there is more of a 'margin for bowyer's error' in a flatter section long bow, and therefore a greater facility for putting it right; e.g. if it is under your ideal draw weight because you have had to correct a twist or tillering error, you can shorten and re-tiller it. (This process may end up a bit like trying to even up the legs of a table, but if the bow ends up on the short side, don't worry –we're aiming to get a finished flatbow of between 62 to 68 inches when measured between nocks).

Having said all that, I have included cutting dimensions for the English longbow for those who wish to go in at the deep end and can obtain wood of suitable quality. These, together with dimensions for other simple bows, are located at the end of this chapter and in chapter 9.

WHICH BOW DESIGN?

The cutting dimensions included in this book allow for some margin for error in a beginner's work. They should produce finished bows of around 50/65lb draw weight, although this depends on the type of wood and how carefully it is tillered. If you have any doubts about the quality of your wood or can't obtain a perfect stave, consider making a wider limbed bow such as the classic 'paddle' or 'pyramid' designs, these can produce very fast, sweet-shooting bows from even the most unpromising of billets.

What poundage?

This is a somewhat inexact science – a bow's finished poundage doesn't only depend on it's physical dimensions, but also on the type of wood, it's grain structure (how it has grown) and quality of tiller. If you start with a long bow with a wide limb, you can always remove material to reduce poundage. To increase poundage you will either have to shorten the bow or add a suitable backing.

'PYRAMID' BOW

A bow with limbs which taper mostly widthways, i.e. at the sides rather than in thickness from back to belly, will significantly reduce stresses and allow you to use more readily available, less costly timbers; it can even accommodate flaws (e.g pins and small knots). String follow is minimised, therefore all those pieces which were rejected as unsuitable for an English longbow can be rescued from the failures box, offcuts bin or rubbish skip, and turned into a traditional bow of true character! Selected spruce and cedar species have been tried (tight growth rings recommended) most being backed for additional safety and longevity. Yew which is unsuitable for an English longbow can make an excellent wide-limbed bow, for example timber from large diameter trees with wide growth rings which are relatively flat, or which has a few flaws.

'PADDLE' BOW

This design, where the bow works hardest is widest part, is another design which can help overcome problems with the wood. The 'Meare Heath' style of bow is an example of a paddle shaped bow; information and cutting dimensions for this type of bow are included in chapter 9.

Recommended bow design basics for initial success

   – don't impose an unsuitable design on a particular piece of wood, or don't select an unsuitable piece of wood for the type of bow you've set your heart on
   – 'rule of thumb' is to make a bow at least twice your drawlength. I recommend 2 1/2 times for a bow with a stiffened handle section
   – bows less than 62 inches should have a more elliptical or segment tiller than longer bows. (See 'tillering' later)

– avoid sudden changes in profile. At the handle, make sure you don't reduce overall cross-sectional area of the limb, i.e. watch your fade-outs, when the limb section becomes shallower, make it wider to compensate

– keep the nocks light. Reinforce them if you are worried about damage from the string loops. Use natural string materials (hemp or linen) if possible, or Dacron with some stretch, because these materials reduce the shock on your bow

– apply a backing to all bows where the grain is breached on the back, or where the limbs are less than 1 1/2inches wide. It depends on the wood and bow design. If in doubt, back it!

– if you are worried about the quality of the wood you are working, make the bow longer and/or wider. It is easy to take wood off, sticking it back on is more complicated.

TO BACK OR NOT TO BACK?
Wide-limbed, flat-section designs reduce stress on the tension side (back) of the limb, provided this stress is evenly spread it reduces the need for a backing; however, you may wish to play safe.
When to consider backing a bow:

– if you have any doubts about the quality of the wood
– when making a bow under 1 1/2inch at its widest point
– when making a short bow (say, under 64 inches)
– if you wish to increase a completed bow's longevity.

There are two choices regarding the stage for backing:

– on the stave before tillering: with a thin lamination of tough wood such as hickory
– on the bow after tillering: with rawhide, textile etc.

A self yew bow with sapwood usually requires no backing, but you must ensure that you follow the grain on the back, I suggest keeping a minimum of 1/4inch of sapwood intact, unless the growth rings are better than 25 per inch, in which case you could reduce this; there is no hard and fast rule, but play safe. A yew bow made from a boughstave, for instance, may have a large proportion of sapwood and you may need more than 1/4inch on the back for it to do it's job, particularly on an English longbow.

Advice on how to apply backings is included later in this chapter: sinew backing is not included because it is a specialised and lengthy process, (the bow takes months to dry properly) and many other fine books and articles exist elsewhere on this topic.

TIMBER

It takes a fair deal of experience to be able to select a suitable tree, fell, store, season and split it with bowmaking in mind, but you have to start somewhere! For those who have the confidence and access to suitable raw material, I have included some guidelines on storing and seasoning bow billets in chapter 9.

BOARDS

It is probably best for the complete beginner to obtain wood from a source of planed timber, so that the grain quality and condition is evident. (Basic timber terms are included in the Glossary.)

Seasoning boards

Ideally bow wood needs to have a stable moisture content suitable for the conditions it is going to be worked in. For preference, boards should be air-dried under cover and outdoors with a good flow of air through well-ordered stacks. If you buy a board which is 'green' you can control seasoning yourself: seal the ends if this hasn't been done, check and turn the board regularly as it dries. The ideal cut for stability in drying is a 'rift' sawn (aka 'edge grain') board of sufficient width. (See Glossary: 'timber terms')

Kiln dried boards

Most boards which are commercially available will be kiln-dried, this is perfectly useable particularly for a flatbow, but may be over-dry; if it has been dried badly (e.g. too quickly) it may have splits and shakes or hidden stresses, all of which can be difficult to spot. A moisture content of 10 to 12 percent is about right, less than that is too dry; if you have the patience store the board outside, laid flat off the ground and under cover for a year or two –it should naturalise to some extent. There are various things to watch out for when visiting suppliers; avoid buying wood from the top of external stockpiles where it has been subjected to weathering extremes, or from enclosed warehouses where the internal temperatures bake the wood dry, or from the bottom of stacks where it may have been lying in a puddle of water for some time. Avoid warped, twisted or badly cupped boards. In any event, if you think the timber is doubtful, make allowances by making a wider-limbed bow.

Which timbers?

There are many species of wood which will make a good bow, all have advantages and disadvantages, unavailability of the very best woods in quantity and quality being the most common. Don't be discouraged by dogma that says you need the perfect piece of wood to make a bow. Be flexible! You can overcome the shortcomings of your chosen billet by selecting a suitable bow design. As I have already said, you greatly increase the list of suitable timbers by choosing a wide-limbed design, you may even discover new species which are suitable –and if someone offers you free timber from a felled tree of a promising nature, consider one of these bows! (See chapter 9)

Some suitable timbers (A non-definitive list)

I have used all these for bowmaking. PLEASE NOTE: some woods cause allergic reactions and many imported timbers are poisonous: all timber dust can cause problems, so please take care.

Ash (English or American white): this is widely available from commercial timberyards and relatively inexpensive; ash has made adequate, and even excellent bows for centuries. American ash generally has straighter grain, English ash can tear if you're not careful to observe the direction of grain. It tends to 'follow the string', so a wide-limb bow is recommended, and/or a longer design.

Bamboo (Cane): strictly speaking this is not timber, but a grass. Victorian longbows were made using this material as a backing, and it is a fine alternative to hickory. When laminating cane, you need to keep as many of the strong external fibre layers as possible, so choose a large diameter cane which can be split into flattish strips. You can leave the nodes intact on the back, or cut through them, but note that the area each side of them is the weakest part. An entire bow made of laminated bamboo is extremely tough but a bit heavy in hand.

Black Walnut: a very attractive wood, easy to work but being dark coloured can hide small pins and knots so select carefully. Back the narrower bows.

Castello Boxwood: this is very similar to lemonwood (later).

False acacia: ('Black locust'): this is an excellent bow wood. English pseudoacacia can follow the string to a relatively large degree; I would recommend that you select it very carefully, and make a wider/longer limbed bow. Consider a backing if the limb is less than 2in. wide.

Elm: if you can find this attractive wood, it makes a fine flatbow. A very good quality piece will make a longbow. Elm is stringy and very difficult to split.

Goncalo Alves: decorative and easy to work, this timber will make an attractive wide-limbed bow.

Greenheart: very dense wood which makes a heavy draw weight bow of small section. Watch out for shakes and splits, as correct seasoning is vital. Dust and splinters can cause poisoning. (Note: it is wise to wear a dust mask when working all woods).

Hickory: while many traditional bowyers discount hickory as a bow-wood, a good piece of hickory will produce an excellent bow, if a little heavy-in-hand, and, with a good piece you can breach the growth rings on the back. Again, it is tough and stringy, and care needs to be taken not to tear the wood while working it.

Laburnum: This makes an excellent bow, but do not retain the sapwood in the finished bow. The sapwood dries quickly, so if you split the log it can pull the heartwood into a useful reflex. (Poisonous)

Lemonwood: nowadays this is not the excellent 'degame' as used in days of yore, the timber imported under this name today is a different species. It is a good dense timber all the same; very easy to work as direction of grain is not critical. Back lemonwood with a strip of hickory if you are making a narrow bow.

Osage orange (historically known as Bois d'arc): like all excellent bow woods, good quality staves are relatively expensive, and it is quite difficult to work. It is tough, and makes an excellent bow, but I don't recommend that you start out with it.

Pequia: a bright yellow wood, similar in character to lemonwood in that it is very easy to work, and makes a good bow. It needs a backing when used in narrow-limbed bows. Can split badly on drying.

Rock maple (Hard maple): used in laminations for fibreglass recurve and flatbow limb cores. It is easily obtained very hard but relatively easy to work, a good sound piece will make a 'self' longbow or flatbow. It is also suitable for backing strips. A good piece allows you to breach the growth rings without penalty! Watch out for splits and cracks, some of which are extremely hard to spot.

Wych elm: the Welsh archers of the Middle Ages used this, and it makes a good bow. It is very tough and stringy, and good quality billets are almost impossible to find!

Yew: easy to work, but really good quality yew for longbows is difficult to find; this is the perfect bow wood for reasons already explained. I wouldn't recommend a beginner sets to work on a top grade piece for an English longbow. Get some practice first! Please note that yew is poisonous: several bowyers are suffering from the effects of it's dust and vapour.

SIZE/NATURE OF BILLET

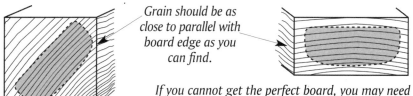

Grain should be as close to parallel with board edge as you can find.

If you cannot get the perfect board, you may need to buy an oversized piece as shown on the left.

PROFILE OF BOW LIMB WITHIN THE WOOD

Ideally, and for simplicity, your first bow should be made from a select piece of wood which has fairly close, even grain which runs parallel for the whole of the required length with no knots, shakes or pins. Life and nature being what it is, this isn't always possible, and if you want true character from your bow, a less than 'perfect' stave is a fine start, you will need to consider amending the design to accommodate any flaws or deviations in grain, e.g. by following a growth ring on the back and/or making a wider limbed bow. Some of the more dense bow woods (e.g. lemonwood) are more accommodating than others regarding changes in grain direction. If the wood isn't perfect, widen the limb and/or lengthen the bow.

For our flatbow:

Select a piece of wood of 72 inches long by 2 inches by 1 1/4 inches; to make things easy for yourself, the grain should run almost parallel with the long dimension (see illustration). If you can't obtain quality wood this long, select a good piece 40 inches in length which is wide enough to be cut to produce two limbs for jointing in the handle (see later). I suggest you take your tape into the timberyard and check all the dimensions as some merchants quote the board size prior to planing, not the actual 'finished size'.

NOTE: You can also make a serviceable wide-limbed bow with the grain running perpendicular to the back, the grain should be as straight as possible and run the length of the bow without deviation (to avoid twisting). Stone age bows have been found with this characteristic.

FOLLOWING THE GRAIN

When looking for your bow wood, you may find a piece with a character which encourages you to consider following the grain on the back of the bow. This procedure can seem daunting to the novice bowmaker, but some woods (e.g. American ash) are quite easy to work down to a single growth

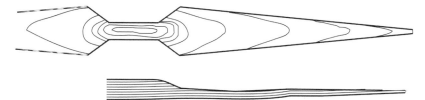

The 'feathering' effect of the growth rings on the belly will vary, according to the taper and density of grain.
The bow above has near parallel limbs so fewer rings will show.

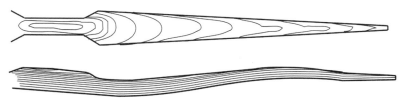

This bow tapers more from belly to back, so more growth rings are visible.
GRAIN PATTERN: BELLY OF BOW: Illustrative examples

ring with a rasp or file; timber with growth rings of 10-15 per inch are recommended. The process may appear time-consuming, but later you will find it easier to work the belly by eye, because the grain will 'feather' towards the nock. It can make a bow of great character, particularly if the grain wanders a little along the bow's length. Mark the selected growth ring for it's full length with pencil before you start, take wood off gradually and renew the pencil mark regularly as you work.

ADHESIVES

Use a good quality powdered resin glue to apply wood backings and glue handle joints, or a good quality two-part epoxy (some of these need heat curing). PVA based glue isn't up to the job. Ensure all surfaces are clean, even, lightly abraded and dust free before gluing. Recommended adhesives for non-wood backings vary: hide glue is recommended for natural materials, impact adhesive for modern flexible materials. (I was once shown a bow which had seat belt material applied as a backing, and very effective it was, too!)

Degreasing

Whatever you are gluing, it is wise to degrease all surfaces to be bonded with acetone or similar. I suggest you put out your cigarette first.

THE TILLER

You will require a piece of strong hardwood to make this; it holds the bow while you to gradually draw it up and 'train' the limbs, it can be clamped

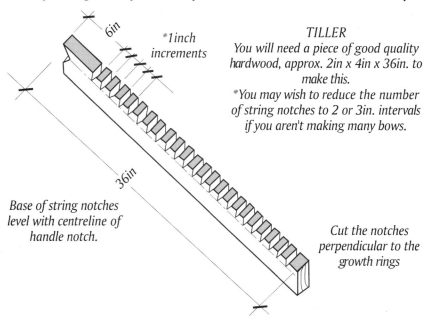

6in

*1inch increments

TILLER
You will need a piece of good quality hardwood, approx. 2in x 4in x 36in. to make this.
You may wish to reduce the number of string notches to 2 or 3in. intervals if you aren't making many bows.

36in

Base of string notches level with centreline of handle notch.

Cut the notches perpendicular to the growth rings

into a 'workmate' type bench to allow you to stand back and assess the limb curvature. More sophisticated versions are bolted to a wall, with ropes and pulleys to help draw up the bow.

TILLERING STRINGS

I suggest you make two tillering strings, both allowing for about 100lb draw weight (the extra strength allows for wear and tear during tillering) the first should be about an inch longer than the proposed bow, for early 'training' of the limbs. The second string should be about two inches shorter than the bow to set an initial bracing height for tillering. You could make an all-purpose adjustable string with a timber hitch on one end, but this knot can slip and/or pull the string (and so the limb) to one side which you want to avoid when training the bow.

FINISHES & FITTINGS

Varnish: e.g. polyurethane, which is tough, and easily repaired.

Handle: braid, suede or buckskin can be used, or cord whipped around the handle, birch bark or fur is truly primitive.

Arrowplate: horn or leather.

Shooting string(s)

BACKINGS

Rawhide backing (optional)

If you can't obtain/afford a whole rawhide skin, suitable rawhide can be obtained by soaking a large knotted bone-shaped dog chew; those 18 inches long produce enough strips to cover both limbs of your average bow. Select a chew with hide about 1/16 to 3/32inch thick if possible, although rawhide can be sanded down on the bow after it has dried. Please note that when soaked, these items can stink, especially when the kind manufacturers put something really 'tasty' for Bonzo in the centre. Soak them outdoors, making sure that neighbourhood dogs are kept away. (This also applies to the completed bow!)

Some other backings which can be applied after tillering.

Vellum, silk, flax, dacron, linen, hemp. These are best applied in a uni-directional fashion, lengthwise on the bow using hide or resin glue. Sinew backing is a specialist and advanced subject –bows backed with this are a serious long-term project, well outside the range of this book!

TOOLS & MATERIALS

You need a very few, basic hand tools to craft your bow. Essential tools are marked with an asterisk.*

*Coarse files/Cabinet makers rasps

Have two or three of these of various grades for different speed of wood removal, flat and half round profiles; you want good quality; there are cheap rasps on the market –keep the handles and throw away the metal bit because the teeth are usually uneven, blunt easily and too widely spaced. A good rasp is a joy to use and will not gouge or tear the wood. A 'millen cut' half round file is excellent if you can get one, but can take a little time to master. Some modern multi-toothed planes are excellent –make sure they are robust.

Drawknife

Not an essential tool, but useful for removing bark and large amounts of material from billets; it must be kept honed to a very fine edge to avoid digging or tearing the wood.

Planes

These are in every workshop, and are useful for removing large amounts of wood in the initial stages; use judiciously though, as it is very easy to get carried away and remove too much!

Scrapers

You can buy cabinet scrapers with a variety of straight, concave and convex shapes, but you can use the back of old sawblade or bandsaw blades, a locknife, old disposable 'Stanley' knife blades (which can be re-sharpened) or even broken glass. I have ground an old saw blade to provide various radii which cover most of the shapes needed for working around wavey grain, knots etc.

Spokeshave

This is not strictly necessary unless you already have one which you are used to using.

A needle rasp or rat-tail file (for the nocks)

If you can't obtain one of these, use a tile saw or a junior-style hacksaw with a wire blade.

Abrasives

Various grades from 60 (for rapid removal) to 150/200 grits for finishing.

Straight edges, carpenters square, measuring tape

These are most useful for initial marking out of cutting dimensions, but over-reliance can discourage bowmakers from using the evidence of their own eyes, which is a good bowmaking skill to develop. Straight edges may help your confidence when you start out but ideally should be a last resort.

Scales

Butcher's or spring scale which reads up to 100lb.

HANDLE JOINTS

If you cannot get a piece of timber of adequate length, you will need to splice two pieces together. 'Book-matched' limbs which are jointed in the handle can make tillering easier, as (hopefully) each limb 'mirrors' the other's curvature. Cut two adjacent pieces from the same board with the grain orientation matched as far as possible. A double fishtail splice is the most strong, or a 'Z' splice, both having a greater surface area than the simple 'V' joint (single fishtail) often suggested. You may need to clamp the limbs onto a board to stop the joint slipping as you clamp it together, alternatively drill through the side of the joint and insert a length of hardwood dowelling.

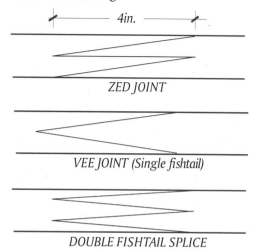

ZED JOINT

VEE JOINT (Single fishtail)

DOUBLE FISHTAIL SPLICE

HANDLE JOINTS

The principle is to provide the maximum surface area in the joint for gluing, therefore the 'zed' and 'double fishtail' joints will be better than the simple 'vee' joint.

APPLYING A WOOD BACKING TO A STAVE

If you are not considering applying rawhide after tillering, or cannot follow the growth rings on the back of your stave because of the way they lie within the board, you may wish to back your stave with a strip of suitable wood before you start any shaping the bow. Good quality hickory, rock maple or bamboo is suitable. Cut (or obtain from a bowyer) a lamination 1/8 to 3/16inch thick; prepare both surfaces for a good, even bond. Abrade and degrease them for good adhesion before applying to the stave using powdered resin or epoxy glue.

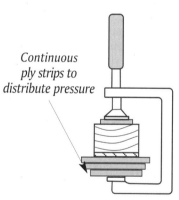

Continuous ply strips to distribute pressure

CLAMPING A WOOD BACKING TO THE STAVE

Clamping

The backing can be bound onto the stave using an old tyre inner tube cut into a long strip and turned around the stave as tightly as you can manage. Clamps provide a more even, reliable pressure and often a better looking joint. Fix clamps at a minimum of 3 inch centres, using long plywood strips between the clamps and wood to help even out the pressure and protect the stave.

1. Marking out and cutting

Carefully mark the centreline on the back of the bow using a chalk line or a long straight edge, and set the other lines out from this. Check it a few times to be sure. You may wish to leave extra width at the nocks to allow for adjustment should a limb twist, or adjust the dimensions if you have a less than 'perfect' stave as already discussed.

2. Rough out the stave

Reduce the stave, with saw or plane, to the outside of the lines.

3. Smooth the back, sides and belly

Round all edges sufficiently to ease bending of the wood, using plane, rasp and file. If there's no backing strip and the grain is suitable, shape the back carefully following a single growth ring of the stave. (See 'following the grain' earlier this chapter).

4. Flexing the bow and 'floor tillering'

Once the bow is flexible, bend each limb by resting the back of the nock end on the floor and pressing down on the handle; this will give you a basic idea of curvature as well as allow you to make a rough assessment of the bow's flexibility and likely draw weight, and whether it is ready for putting on the tiller; you can also determine if one limb is much more stiff than the other. This is only a rough method, the remaining work is done on the tiller.

5. Shaping

Some important points to remember when shaping the bow:

– avoid sudden changes in profile

– work out all tool marks, particularly gouges/sawlines before tillering, paying special attention to the back of the bow

– leave a raised area of wood around pins or knots to strengthen them (see illustration)

– keep the back particularly smooth and toolmark free

– regularly squint down the stave to check for any sudden changes in direction

– don't rush it! Brew tea or coffee regularly, and if you get tired and/or confused, take a long break

– use a tool suitable for the job in hand: a rasp is a little drastic if you just want to take a couple of pounds off the draw weight!

– avoid sharp edges; round arrises and keep all changes in profile smooth and gradual, remember that a curved surface bends more easily and sharp internal corners can fracture.

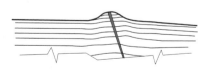

Small pins and knots can be reinforced by leaving protective wood around them. Soft knots should be drilled out and a hardwood dowel plug (traditionally known as a 'Dutchman') glued in place.

TILLERING
Take your time.

Many a good stave has been ruined by tillering it too quickly. If one limb has a weakness and the bow is drawn up too far, you will have a potential weak spot in the bow, where it can ultimately break or collapse even if the wood fibres have not visibly chrysalled. A bow may take a large 'set' if tillered too quickly, or one limb may weaken and 'unbalance' the bow. Wood needs to be gradually trained to the curvature. You can knock pounds in draw weight off a bow and lose potential cast by tillering it too quickly and carelessly. As you work the bow, flex it often while checking it constantly for straightness and tiller.

INITIAL STRINGING
Cut temporary stringing nocks in the sides of the limb, (avoid cutting into the back of the bow) and attach the tillering string. Secure the bow in its notch in the tiller, and gradually draw it up a few inches, flexing it many times (at least 30) for each inch increase in draw, while watching for any stiff points. Remove wood carefully as necessary until you have the bow coming round evenly and sufficiently to fit the shorter string, which should give you around a 4inch bracing height. (You may wish to use the temporary nocks for a stringer, and cut another set inside these for the shorter string.)

Brace the bow to about 4inches.

Now check the bow for tiller and straightness. Squint down the bow from both ends, and lay it on it's back and check the position of the string; if it bisects the handle, and the limbs aren't twisted, you have an excellent start. If one limb is far too stiff, remove wood as necessary to create an equal bend before drawing the bow up further. If you don't trust your eyesight, you can measure this (see illustration later) this is a good checking procedure for the insecure, but primitive style self bows don't necessarily require this degree of accuracy, particularly the more 'snakey' staves. If the string doesn't bisect the handle don't worry, as it's early days yet! (See the section on 'Twisting' later).

TILLERED PROFILE (See illustrations)
Now for some basics regarding limb curvature. For our long-ish bow, you should be aiming for an even bend starting about 3 to 6 inches above the handle, and stopping about 4 to 6 inches from the limb tip; exact dimensions aren't rigidly set, and vary according to overall bow length. A bow which comes round at the limb tips (i.e. too whip-ended) is not ideal and will be inclined to stack, this is usually not a major weakness, whereas a 'hinge' mid-limb is more of a problem. The shorter the bow (also the lighter the draw weight) the more tricky good tillering becomes. If the bow is shorter than 62 inches between nocks, you will need more of an

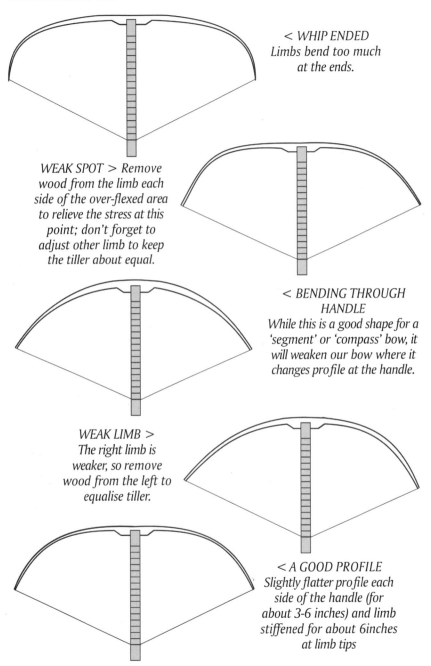

< WHIP ENDED
Limbs bend too much
at the ends.

WEAK SPOT > Remove
wood from the limb each
side of the over-flexed area
to relieve the stress at this
point; don't forget to
adjust other limb to keep
the tiller about equal.

< BENDING THROUGH
HANDLE
While this is a good shape for a
'segment' or 'compass' bow, it
will weaken our bow where it
changes profile at the handle.

WEAK LIMB >
The right limb is
weaker, so remove
wood from the left to
equalise tiller.

< A GOOD PROFILE
Slightly flatter profile each
side of the handle (for
about 3-6 inches) and limb
stiffened for about 6inches
at limb tips

TILLERING THE LIMBS: BOW PROFILE

'elliptical tiller', that is some degree of bend through the handle (the bow will be said to 'work through the handle'); in this instance carefully reduce the handle depth to reduce stress on the limbs at the change of profile –you can pack out the grip for comfort on completion. For shorter bows you should consider a 'segment' bow, which forms an arc at full draw.

Continue tillering and checking for straightness, shaping the handle as you progress. As the bow reduces in draw weight you must be more careful in removing wood as each shaving will have proportionately more effect on the bow tiller and draw weight. You will eventually get to the point where you can come up to full draw with the ideal tiller, and you will have some idea of whether the draw weight is manageable.

You may wish to make the stiffer limb the lower one; in this case, allow for a 1/8 to 1/4inch difference in limb tiller as illustrated below. (Note: some 'primitive' staves may shoot better the 'wrong way up': see later)

Take both measurements at mid-limb and 3in. either side.

LIMB TILLER

The lower limb can be made stiffer than the upper, as it is under more stress in drawing up.

IF YOUR BOW IS TWISTING

Firstly, relax.

A twisted bow can shoot perfectly well and a modicum of twist is not a disaster. If the bow is 'propellored' yet the string still lies within the handle as you look down it, the bow is fine, believe me. You are making a singular bow with character, not a perfectly engineered specimen for the perfectionist to admire. If the twist is minor, you can work it out as you train the bow round to it's finished profile; as long as the string lies within the handle, the twist is not a major problem. The earlier you can correct a serious twist the better –continuing to 'train' the wood while it is in this state can make the situation worse. If you feel the bow twist in your hand as you draw it, then it needs early correction.

WHY BOWS CAN TWIST

1. Too much wood on one side of the limb

Limbs generally twist towards the weaker side of the bow. If the whole bow is twisted then the problem may be around the handle section, if one limb is twisted, then it is more localised.

2. Natural stresses within the stave.

Sometimes the way the stave has grown in the tree, variations in grain, flaws or the way it has been dried causes stresses within it that are just making it 'contrary'; this is also likely if the grain 'runs off' to the side of the stave. Some knots side shoots or damage during growth can also have this effect. Sometimes you cannot completely overcome this.

CORRECTING TWIST
At the limbs

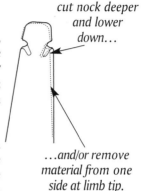

cut nock deeper and lower down...

Remove wood gradually from the stronger side, removing material from the side and belly of the limb; flex the bow gently to encourage the bow to come round before re-checking for twist; remember to regularly check the curvature on the tiller.

At the nocks

If the above method is not adequate, you can deepen the nock on the side towards which the bow is twisting, and/or cut it lower down the limb. If you left extra width on the limb tips when marking out, you can remove material at the limb ends on the relevant side to help bring the limb round.

...and/or remove material from one side at limb tip.

One way to help correct limb twist

To correct a twist you will probably need to use a combination of these methods; try to carry out any adjustments gradually.

DRAW WEIGHT

A bow will lose draw weight after it has been 'shot in', so allow about 5lb over. A bow will also lose poundage if it is overdrawn, so tiller it to your drawlength and no further. The lighter your bow becomes, the more effect the removal of each shaving, so be cautious. If you feel the bow is far too light, you can shorten (or 'pike') it. Do this a little at a time, working on both limbs equally, and always re-check the tiller and curvature before coming to full draw. Once you have settled on the bow's length make the final string, and brace the bow to the finished bracing height which I suggest is between 6 and 7 inches for a 70 inch bow. Tiller the bow to its final drawlength. You are now ready for test shooting.

TEST SHOOTING

Try arrows of various spines and weights: if they don't fly well and if all else fails, try the bow the other way up! I made an Osage self bow from a snakey stave whose character 'dictated' (so I thought) which should be the lower limb as it was deflexed, but no arrows came out sweetly whatever I tried. Turned the other way up, it was forgiving and silent; it didn't conform with the conventional 'tiller' as the lower limb came round visibly more than the top. I toyed with the idea of adjusting it but many shoots later and, untouched by scraper since, it has become my favourite. It is sweet to draw, forgiving and plenty fast enough, so all comments that it's 'out of tiller' get ignored!

After a few dozen arrows, inspect the bow thoroughly: check the tiller, straightness, brace height etc. and adjust if necessary. Then shoot some more and re-check until you are satisfied that the bow is standing up well. After several dozen arrows, the bow may drop further in draw weight, so you may want to check this too.

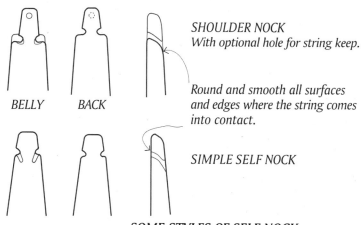

SHOULDER NOCK
With optional hole for string keep.

Round and smooth all surfaces and edges where the string comes into contact.

BELLY   BACK

SIMPLE SELF NOCK

SOME STYLES OF SELF NOCK

SHAPING/STRENGTHENING THE NOCKS

There are a number of ways of finishing bow nocks, from the simple angled groove to gluing on a decorative piece of hardwood. In all cases the area where the string touches must be smooth. If the nock is particularly small, you can glue and bind on a wedge as illustrated.

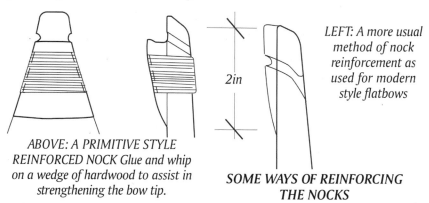

LEFT: A more usual method of nock reinforcement as used for modern style flatbows

2in

ABOVE: A PRIMITIVE STYLE REINFORCED NOCK Glue and whip on a wedge of hardwood to assist in strengthening the bow tip.

SOME WAYS OF REINFORCING THE NOCKS

APPLYING A RAWHIDE BACKING

This is best applied after the bow is tillered. If the bow has followed the string you may wish to clamp the bow to a reflexed former or in a jig when applying the backing, which will give it a degree of reflex. This may also add a few pounds to the draw weight.

Hide glues

These are recommended for rawhide and sinew backings, being flexible and strong, if a little messy to use –get the finest you can afford. I use a mix of pearl glue and size with a very small amount of rabbit skin glue granules. Hide glue should not be boiled, but heated gradually and enough water restored as it evaporates to maintain the consistency of single cream. Liquid hide glue is also available, but it takes a long time to dry; I have read that if you add a little vinegar to it this speeds things up, but I haven't tried it myself.

Preparing the rawhide.

The rawhide will need to be soaked for several hours to soften, then trim the strips so that they lap slightly round the sides of the limbs. While you are heating the glue/water mixture take your soaked rawhide, and place it in hot water (not too hot as you will end up with what looks like pork scratchings!)

Preparing the bow

Degrease and lightly abrade the back of the bow –also warm the back if possible just before applying the glue. Apply a generous amount of glue to the bow, lay the hide on the back and quickly bind around the two with string, each turn approx. 1/8inch apart. Spring clips can help hold the hide in place as you do this. String can leave ridges on the backing, so you may prefer to use crepe bandage.

'Curing'

Lay the bow flat and leave it to dry slowly and naturally for several days in a heated room (preferably not over a source of direct heat). When you have removed the binding, even up the edges of the hide with a file or coarse abrasive, and remove any 'grooving' effect left by the binding. Check the bow's tiller, drawing it up slowly and gently; reduce the thickness of the backing if necessary with file and abrasives.

Protecting the hide

Rawhide will react to moisture and soften, as will hide glues, so you need to apply a good waterproof finish. Add decoration if you fancy it: I add genuine earth pigments to the varnish for that natural primitive look! Polyurethane varnishes are fine for the job and easy to apply.

ARROW PLATE

If you choose to fit one, this should be hardwearing or easily replaceable (e.g. horn, leather, ivory, mother-of-pearl); recess it if possible, ensuring that it is actually located where the arrow passes on the bow.

FINISHING

Ensure that all gouges and tool marks are completely smoothed out, particularly on the back, and all edges rounded. Clean off the dust and degrease the surface before applying your chosen finish. A good quality applied finish will not only waterproof the bow but will bring out the beauty of the grain; polyurethane lacquer is cheap, tough, waterproof and easy to patch after an argument with a bramble bush. Other, even hardier finishes are available but aren't so cheap or easy to use. I apply several thin coats, rubbing down between the last three, then wait a few days to ensure it has cured before applying a modern silicone polish.

Natural finishes: if you prefer a natural finish more consistent with your primitive bow, natural oils are recommended; Tung oil will bring out the colour and highlight the grain; alternatively a modern blended finishing oil dries more rapidly and also enhances the beauty of the wood. While these finishes aren't as tough as polyurethane varnish, they are easily repaired and maintained.

HANDLE

You may wish to pack the handle to a rounded shape to suit your hand with tape or a wood or cork packer (see later); for a grip you can use string binding, braid or leather binding, or if you wish to be truly primitive, birch bark, stitched hide or animal fur.

THE ENGLISH LONGBOW: additional notes.

A few additional pointers on making this type of bow:

– the wood is under more stress due to the deeper limb section so greater care in selection of the wood is required

–you have to be additionally careful in tillering; an English longbow is more inclined to fret and twist because it has narrower, 'stacked' limbs

–always keep the limb a little wider than its depth, to help reduce potential twisting problems

–try and start with a longer bowstave (say, 76 inches) and work your way down

– if you're worried about twisting limbs or the accuracy of your marking out, keep the nocks a little wider than the 1/2inch indicated in the cutting dimensions, this will allow for extra adjustment

–the British Long-Bow Society requires horn nocks for most of it's competitions, and has a specific minimum limb width to depth ratio and bow length to drawlength dimensions. (See Glossary)

–tillering is similar to that for the flatbow, though profiles can vary from a 'compass' bow to the 'butt' (target) profile with handle dips as illustrated in the cutting dimensions.

Marking out the English longbow

This needs considerable care, as there is less margin for error. Measure two or three times before you cut!

Avoiding that sideways twist

If a longbow starts to twist it is most likely because the limb is too narrow in relation to it's depth. Keep the limb a little wider (1/16 to 1/8inch) than it is deep –so err on the side of caution until you have trained the bow. Once you have braced and drawn the bow far enough to be sure it is not twisting you can reduce poundage by carefully removing a little material from the sides as well as the belly.

Method

Roughing out, smoothing the edges and back, tillering and 'training' the bow is exactly as for the flatbow already described, bearing in mind the additional pointers which started this section.

HORN NOCKS
Fitting the nocks.

Unless you have a very steady hand or don't mind potentially ruining hours of work, the nocks should be 90% shaped before fitting them to the bow. Cut a length of horn and drill it with a tapered hole (you can use a modified 10mm flatbit) and glue the horn sections onto lengths of dowel, using either a low temperature hot melt which can be released with a heat gun, or a water-based glue that can be soaked off. This makes it easy to hold the nocks in a vice for filing and rasping, or grip in your hand when using a sander (you may find a belt or disc sander useful to remove material quickly if you already have one).

When shaping the nocks:

–ensure that the tip of the stave is behind the string (and stringer) groove

–provide a smooth transition between the back of the bow and the nock, this is necessary for easy stringing

–the string grooves should be deep enough to hold the string, but not too deep (particularly in the top nock) so that you cannot unbrace the bow without a struggle

–your string loops should be sized to match your nocks: too large and they may slip out of the groove or twist the bow, too tight and unstringing can become a battle of wills which could mean the end of your bow.

The bow tips should be tapered for around 1 to1 1/2 inches to fit behind the string and stringer grooves as illustrated. Glue the nocks using a good quality epoxy resin; you can stop the nocks 'popping' off the bow before this has set by stringing the bow at a low bracing height until it has cured, this also allows you to check that the nocks are aligned correctly.

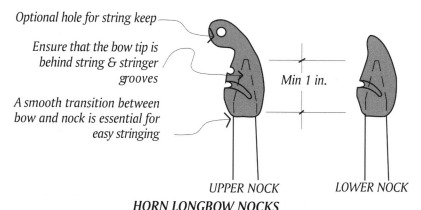

Optional hole for string keep

Ensure that the bow tip is
behind string & stringer
grooves

A smooth transition between
bow and nock is essential for
easy stringing

Min 1 in.

UPPER NOCK   LOWER NOCK

HORN LONGBOW NOCKS
A traditional style is illustrated here

Polishing horn nocks

This is a labour of love, using increasingly fine abrasives to get a smooth
finish and a fine lustre: for finishing off the nocks there are special polishes
available from horn suppliers, but very fine steel wool (Grade 0000) elbow
grease and a good wax polish, well burnished, gives a good finish.

Packing the handle

Some bows will require an additional piece of shaped softwood packing on
the back to 'round' the handle for comfort. If the bow bends through the
handle, saw slots in the packer as shown to help the packer flex with the
bow. Alternatively cork makes an excellent and more flexible packer which
is particularly useful if the bow works through the handle. I find it useful
to wrap cloth tape around the handle before applying a braid, cord or
leather grip.

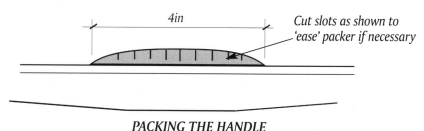

4in

Cut slots as shown to
'ease' packer if necessary

PACKING THE HANDLE

85

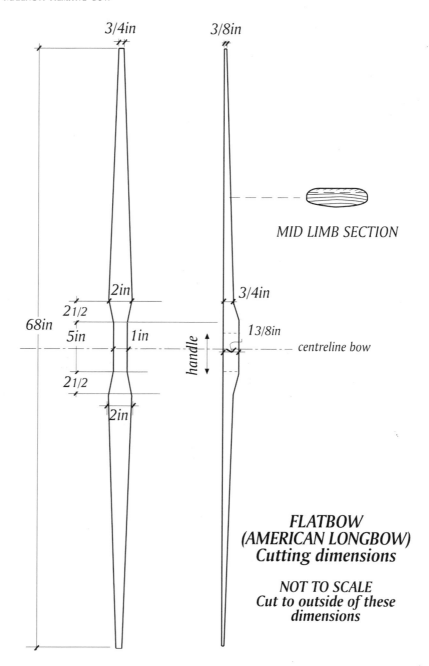

3/4in

3/8in

MID LIMB SECTION

2in

3/4in

2 1/2

68in

5in 1in

13/8in

centreline bow

handle

2 1/2

2in

**FLATBOW
(AMERICAN LONGBOW)
Cutting dimensions**

*NOT TO SCALE
Cut to outside of these
dimensions*

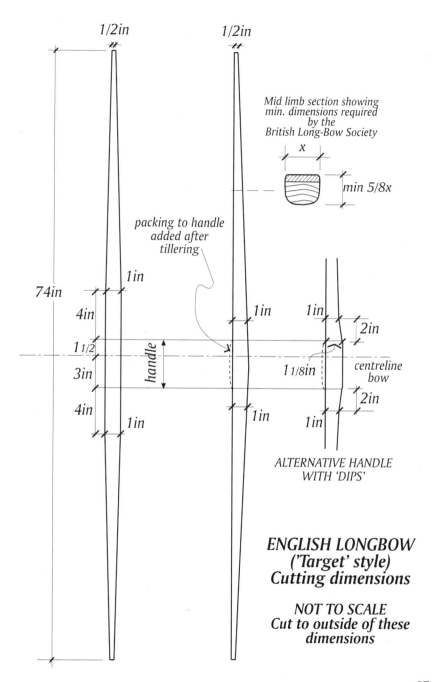

1/2in

1/2in

Mid limb section showing
min. dimensions required
by the
British Long-Bow Society

x

min 5/8x

packing to handle
added after
tillering

74in

1in

4in

1in

1in

1 1/2

handle

3in

1 1/8in

centreline
bow

4in

1in

2in

2in

ALTERNATIVE HANDLE
WITH 'DIPS'

**ENGLISH LONGBOW
('Target' style)
Cutting dimensions**

**NOT TO SCALE
Cut to outside of these
dimensions**

87

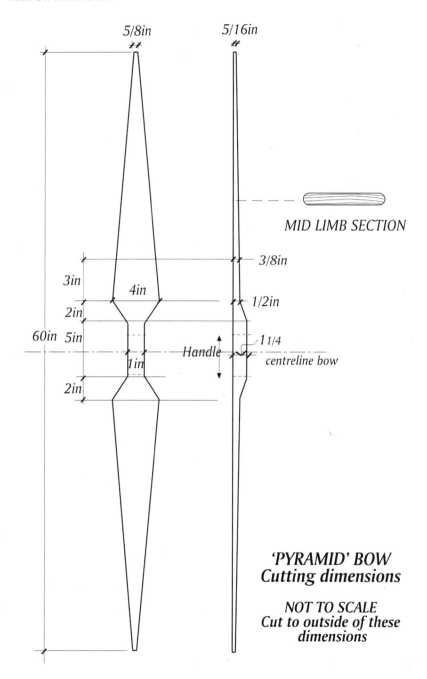

5/8in

5/16in

MID LIMB SECTION

3/8in

3in

4in

1/2in

60in   5in

Handle   1 1/4

centreline bow

2in

1in

2in

'PYRAMID' BOW
Cutting dimensions

NOT TO SCALE
*Cut to outside of these
dimensions*

9. MORE HISTORIC (& PREHISTORIC) BOW DESIGNS

The three types of bow described in this chapter are based on historic and archaeological artefacts which could be termed 'primitive' bows, as defined at the start of this book – bows made from natural materials which shoot around the handle, but which don't meet the generally accepted criteria for the English longbow. Bows from prehistory are far from primitive in design; early bowmakers would have pushed the available technology to it's limits, much like those of today, and I'm sure that the special relationship modern-day archers have with their traditional bows is something which the maker of the Meare Heath would have recognised 4,500 years ago! The fundamentals of bowmaking remain as set out in Chapter 8, so I will try not to repeat myself, but instead draw your attention any additional factors or changes in approach particular to the design being described.

RAW MATERIAL
There are many variables involved in felling, seasoning and drying timber for bows; if you have access to a suitable log or someone offers a tree for the purpose, the following basic guide may help.

Seasoning basics
The length of time it takes to season timber is affected by:
   – the species of timber involved
   – the season in which it is felled: there are various theories about the best time to fell timber in order to control moisture content: some bowmakers consider spring the best time for cutting yew
   – the climate in which it is seasoned.

Moisture content and shrinkage
The degree of shrinkage of a piece of timber during drying depends on the species and how the drying is carried out and controlled: for example kiln-dried black locust (*pseudoacacia*) will shrink volumetrically by 10%, some species of hickory by 17%. In 'green' wood the moisture content of the sapwood and hardwood will be different; usually sapwood is wetter, but not always– for example some oaks and hickories are different.

Equilibrium moisture content
Ideally you need to dry the timber to a stable level for the climate in which it is to be worked and used. If you decide to season it by air drying, the rule of thumb is one year air drying for each inch of timber thickness, but this varies according to species and the conditions in which it is stored. If you are going to make several bows using a variety of woods, I recommend that you obtain an electronic moisture meter (there are some makes which don't rely on pins driven into the wood); ensure it gives a reading from a suitable depth for your average bow billet (minimum 1 1/2-2 inches); you can start working the wood when it reads around 13 to14% in the UK.

Seasoning bow timber

To reduce the many variables that can spoil a stave, try to ensure the timber is adequately seasoned before you start working it. Bows made from 'green' wood will tend to follow the string and can warp and split as they dry; very wet wood split into bow billets too early and dried too quickly can also twist and split for similar reasons and you need to consider carefully the risks if you do this. Very large logs will need to be split for transporting. A basic guide to seasoning follows:

– prepare the timber before storing: seal both cut ends as soon as possible and any bark damage with waterproof sealant; store billets under cover with a good flow of air all 'round, e.g. in an unheated and well ventilated shed; stack the wood off the ground; ensure it is well and evenly supported; seal the pith of split green wood, particularly yew.

– turn the wood regularly; this helps it dry evenly and you can also check for insect damage etc.

– avoid storing timber where it is subjected to sudden extremes of heat or cold which cause stresses in drying resulting in shakes or splits. If seasoning indoors the room should be unheated and of fairly constant temperature. A roof void is usually a bad storage area for this reason.

Splitting the log

Spend as much time as you can assessing the way the wood lies in the billet. Turn the log over in your hand and mind considering the following:

– one side of the log may have fewer pins and knots than the other, depending on which side was in the sun or most protected.

– the grain at the base of the tree will be unsuitable, so discount this part when calculating the length.

– is the log warped? The reflex side may be more useful.

– look at both ends of the log to see where the growth rings go: are they wider one side than the other? This may indicate stresses within the wood; growth rings in your bowstave should be as consistently even as possible.

– avoid twisted growth or 'reaction wood' (e.g. where the tree has developed with increased compression on one side due to growing on the side of a slope or bank).

– some woods split more readily than others, elm is particularly tough, for instance.

– if the wood is already split at one point it is telling you something!

– try and visualise your bow within the wood, checking the required clear length in relation to knots and pins etc. A tape measure and chalk may help you here.

A perfect bowstave in nature is a rare thing, so be prepared to compromise –the challenge here is to make a suitable bow out of the wood available.

BOW DESIGNS: (PRE-HISTORY IN THE MAKING)

1. THE MEARE HEATH TYPE

I spent some hours in the company of this bow, and realised just why it is considered something special by archaeologists and archers alike. The design is a variant of the paddle bow and so is suitable for a variety of woods, however to help ensure pre-history isn't repeated, I have suggested some minor amendments to the original design.

The artefact and a brief history

The find is half a bow made of yew, which has broken in the handle. It was buried in the peat of the Somerset levels in the west of England and has been carbon-dated to around 2,500BC (Neolithic). Within a few miles of this bow another, smaller yew half-bow was found, also broken in the handle and similarly preserved in the peat; this bow was of a completely different design, having a narrow 'D' limb profile (as the English longbow section) this artefact was dated to within 100 years of the Meare Heath, and is known as the 'Ashcott' bow. Also found in the same area are many timber tracks, a testament to the engineering skills of our ancestors who built them to ease crossing of the marshes between their settlements on higher ground; near to these tracks have been found 'offerings' of unused axeheads made from valuable imported stone, and it is possible that the broken bows in this area were similar offerings.

Description

The Meare Heath bow has very wide, shallow limbs, approx. 62mm x 17mm (2 1/2in. x 3/4in.) and a narrow handle with a distinctive 'keel' profile this has a relatively short fadeout into the belly of the bow, part of the keel has 'blown off' the belly during breakage, indicating a possible weakness in transition between handle and limb cross sections which could have been the reason for failure.

There are decorative bindings on the bow:

Lateral strips of oxhide which have been scarf jointed on the back, two of these remain; the wider has been slashed parallel with the long edge with very fine flint tool. Marks indicate there were possibly 8 such bindings.

Diagonal binding : a fragment remains (material unidentified but animal in origin); marks indicate this binding criss-crossed the length of the limb.

Several sharp tool marks scarring the back of the bow indicate that the bindings were applied after the working bow was complete. The bow has followed the string very slightly.

The nock is of a 'button' type (the Ashcott bow nock is similar) and has been reinforced with binding to the end of the limb, only slight marks of which remain.

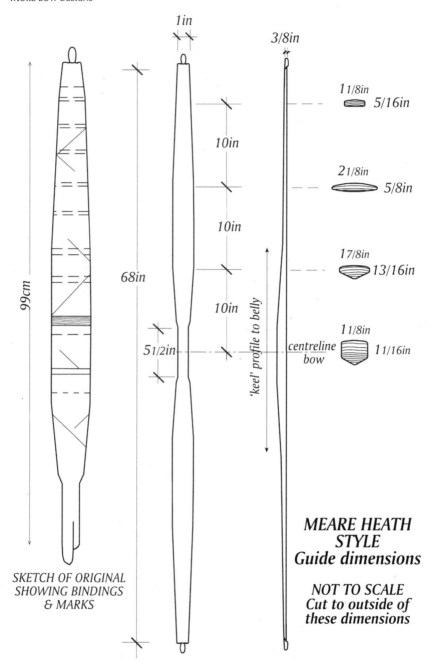

99cm

68in

1in

10in

10in

10in

5 1/2in

3/8in

'keel' profile to belly

centreline
bow

1 1/8in
5/16in

2 1/8in
5/8in

1 7/8in
13/16in

1 1/8in
1 1/16in

SKETCH OF ORIGINAL
SHOWING BINDINGS
& MARKS

**MEARE HEATH
STYLE
Guide dimensions**

**NOT TO SCALE
Cut to outside of
these dimensions**

The wood: there is no sign of sapwood having been retained on the back; the yew is evenly grained, density better than 25 rings/inch, clean and knot free –a fine piece for a time when pollen studies indicate yew was very scarce in the area. The centre of the heartwood is offset in the bow but there is no obvious sign of this having caused the bow to twist.

PRACTICAL TIPS ON MAKING A MEARE HEATH STYLE BOW
Draw weight
It is impossible to assess the true draw-weight of the original bow, but approximations I have made vary from 70 to 95 lb at a modern archers drawlength of 28 inches. The cutting dimensions I have given should produce a bow around 50-60lb draw weight at 28 inches, but as always, wood is so variable (yew in particular) it would be wise to start on the large/long side and work your way down as necessary. I have made this type of bow in American cherry, English yew and rock maple.

Length and longevity
Having just half a bow is a problem and there is nothing to suggest that Neolithic people were obsessed with symmetry; if the original bow *was* symmetrical, it would have been around 5 feet 6 inches long; I suggest you use the 'rule of thumb' regarding length of your bow, making it 2 1/4 to 2 1/2 times your drawlength.

Fadeouts
If you have no wish to sacrifice your hard work, I suggest you widen the handle slightly and lengthen the keel to the fadeout somewhat (similar to the dimensions I have given).

Backing and decoration
A bow of this width should not need a backing, but if you have any doubts about the quality of the wood, I suggest you play safe and apply rawhide or similar. If you are using yew, I suggest you leave some sapwood on the back; although the original shows no sign of our forbears having retained the sapwood, we are making an approximation, not a replica. It has been observed that the pale colour of the back indicates the rings just beneath the sapwood were retained: it is difficult to be certain about this because of the age of the piece and it's subsequent preservation in Carbowax. The decorative bindings should not affect the bow's performance unless they are too loose and flap about.

String and nocks
The part of the top nock which remains indicates an elongated button type, with strengthening bindings applied below this, probably to protect the soft yew from excessive bruising or splitting by the string as well as providing more decoration. I recommend you reinforce the nocks in a similar manner. It is likely that the original string was of vegetable fibres, similar to the linen or hemp strings of today: a sinew string would have softened considerably in the moist air of the region.

2. A CABLE BACKED BOW

Imagine the scene...

Temperatures well below zero and not a tree in sight. You have poor quality staves obtained from barrels or cases imported into the Trading Posts. Baleen and bone are available, but animal or resin based glues don't work reliably in this climate; temperatures make wood brittle and prone to fly apart under strain. You need a bow, but what do you do?...

Use your skills in in cordage and knotwork, that's what –and the Inuit and Siberian tribes of the frozen plains were masters of these arts. A sinew cable on the back of a bow acts in a similar way as a glued backing by modifying the neutral axis and relieving tensile stresses on the back of a bow. In addition transverse knots holding the cables in place tighten as the bow is drawn up, clamping the fibres together. There are sophisticated examples of these bows in the Smithsonian Institute, their knotwork is fantastic and complex. (I recommend you read the report by John Murdoch in the Report of the US National Museum 1884: "A study of the Eskimo bows in the US National Museum")

It is great fun to try your hand at making a cable bow, they shoot very well, and for the inveterate tinkerer taking them apart for adjustment is easy –no glues! They shoot extremely well; I have a very short acacia 'segment' profiled flatbow (it forms a near perfect arc at full draw): 57 inches from nock to nock and far from the best example of this timber: it draws 27 inches and shoots extremely quickly. Another example I made from birch has chrysalled it's entire length but has not collapsed or broken because of the cable backing –it still shoots well. I suggest you use a wood which is not too soft, as the cord could compress the wood fibres and slip rather than grip where it is knotted around the limb..

The practicalities

Some modifications are needed to the flatbow design to allow for the fitting of the cable:

- ideally the bow should have a 'segment' profile rather than a stiffened handle
- make the nocks wider and more substantial in order to take the cable as well as the string
- try to eliminate twist and keep the handle fairly wide in order to prevent the cable slipping off sideways: you can correct this tendency to a certain extent by tying the cable to the limb, but it is simpler to reduce this problem early on.

If you are applying a cable because you are more worried about the quality of the wood than sub-zero temperatures, tiller the bow to 1/2 to 2/3 of your final drawlength before fitting the cable; this should ensure that the basic tillering is okay without risking the bow.

Cable material

Dacron is suitable and hardwearing; linen can be used, but wears out quite quickly –the main problem is that most natural materials can chafe, particularly if you have put knots in the length of the bow, but at least they are easy to replace on a cable bow! There really is no adequate substitute for sinew, but you may find preparing enough of this to rope together into many feet of cable a bit tiresome. Whatever yarn you use, wax it well during manufacture and application to the bow.

FITTING THE CABLE

Before you start to fit the cable you will need to make a 'toggle' to wind the string, as illustrated. Two toggles are even more useful, They should be thin but strong enough to grip and turn the cable: the originals were bone, but I have used hard maple with success: smooth and polish it well so that it does not scratch the back of the bow.

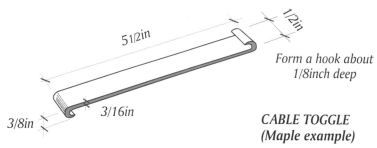

51/2in

1/2in

Form a hook about 1/8inch deep

3/8in   3/16in

**CABLE TOGGLE
(Maple example)**

The backing cable will stretch, so it is useful to put temporary reflex into the bow before applying the cable; this will help take stretch out of the cord as you wind it around the nocks. I have made a jig as illustrated.

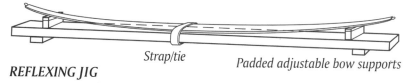

Strap/tie

REFLEXING JIG   *Padded adjustable bow supports*

There are several ways of attaching a cable and you need to decide which is the most appropriate for your stave and design: I recommend you tie the start of the cord securely at the handle with a temporary knot and once you have finished winding the cable, join this to the end of the cord with a secure knot: this join will then be bound and further secured when you bind the cable to the handle.

The simple nock to nock method

Tie the cord securely to the handle and wind 20 or more strands of cable (i.e. 10+ per side) between the nocks, pulling the material as tight as possible to maintain even tension and reduce stretch; tie it off securely to

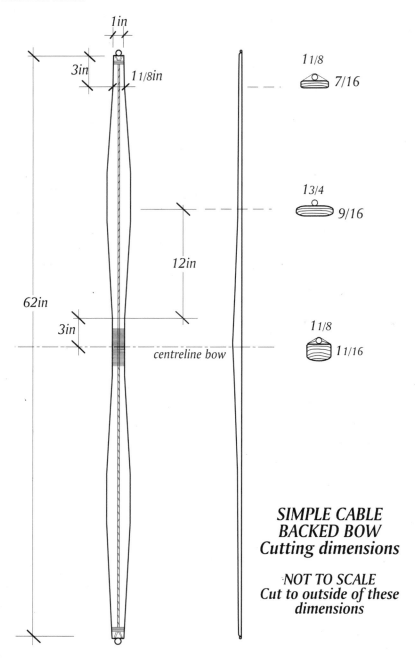

1in

3in

1 1/8in

62in

3in

12in

centreline bow

1 1/8
7/16

1 3/4
9/16

1 1/8
1 1/16

SIMPLE CABLE
BACKED BOW
Cutting dimensions

NOT TO SCALE
Cut to outside of these
dimensions

the starting end at the handle. If you wish to strengthen the stave with binding mid-limb, I have illustrated two types of knot.

The mid-knot

This knot is formed mid limb and the cord carried up round the nock, then down over the top of the knot, form the knot around the other limb, then carry the cord on to that nock and back again, each knot you make traps the previous loop of cord as indicated.

The end knot

This ties a cable between the limbs rather than the nocks and is useful for reinforcing the limbs and stiffening the central section of the bow.

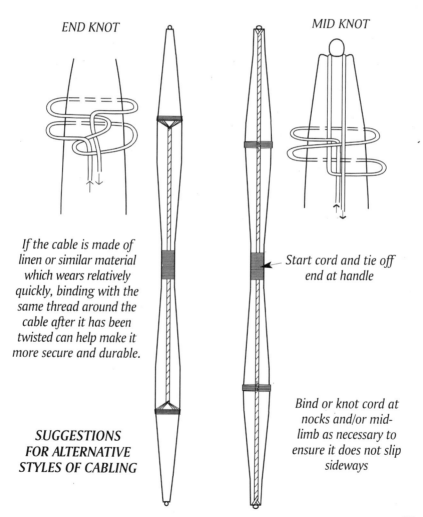

END KNOT

MID KNOT

If the cable is made of linen or similar material which wears relatively quickly, binding with the same thread around the cable after it has been twisted can help make it more secure and durable.

Start cord and tie off end at handle

SUGGESTIONS FOR ALTERNATIVE STYLES OF CABLING

Bind or knot cord at nocks and/or mid-limb as necessary to ensure it does not slip sideways

Winding the cable

Remove the bow from the reflex jig. Insert the toggle between the two main strands of cable at the handle and start winding, hooking the cable, turning and pulling the toggle through; 30 times will do, initially. If you have knotted the cable at the mid-limb as well as at the nocks, you will need to wind all three sections of cable separately, you can experiment by making some sections more taut than others. Leave the toggle(s) in place and temporarily clip or tie them to prevent unwinding. Flex the bow a few times to stretch the cable, don't pull to full draw as the cable is not secured and may slip sideways: wind it up a few more times. I have wound Dacron cable on a 58 inch bow over 45 times, sufficient to lift the nocks over 1inch, after full draw this stretched but resulted in a good, taught cable.

Replace the toggle with a temporary tie to hold the cable in place (I use plastic cable clips). You can now string the bow and draw it up a little more. Continue doing this until you are up to full draw. Wind the cable more if you like: experiment with the effect this has on the bow tiller, profile and draw weight.

Once you are satisfied the cable is doing it's job, you can use the toggles to hold the cable while you tie one ply of the cable onto the bow at the nocks and handle as illustrated, using the same material used for the cable itself; I use a blunt darning needle to simplify things. Remove the toggles and bind over the whole cable at the handle.

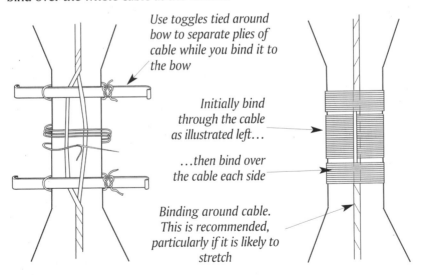

Use toggles tied around bow to separate plies of cable while you bind it to the bow

Initially bind through the cable as illustrated left...

...then bind over the cable each side

Binding around cable. This is recommended, particularly if it is likely to stretch

BINDING CABLE AT HANDLE

Additional binding at the nocks, if required, can be carried out in a similar way

HOLMEGAARD STYLE

There are several examples of this design from Denmark, spanning a 3,000 year period, with some variations in width length etc. between them; one particular bow which is largely complete (apart from a missing tip) has been the model for many approximations. Flemming Alrune's writings on this remarkable style of bow inspired me to turn a piece of English elm into a 'working model' which shoots extremely well –the bow is light in hand, sweet to draw and very fast-shooting; this is the bow I have used for the cutting dimensions given later in this chapter.

The artefact

Found in the bogs of the lowlands of Denmark, one example is 9,000 years old; and is in four pieces. The area in which it was found would have been heavily forested at the time it was made. The bow cross section changes markedly approximately halfway along the limbs, from a flat, wide design near the handle to a deeper, narrower profile towards the nock; the bow has a rounded back and appears to have been made from a piece of clean elm of approximately 2 inches diameter. The back follows the growth rings so exactly it is likely that the bowstave was unmodified apart from removal of the bark.

– approximate length 60 to 62 inches overall (1540mm)
– the handle is approximately 11/8in. square (27mm) and the limbs at their widest 15/8inches in width (42mm) by 11/16inch deep (20mm)
– draw weight is impossible to determine accurately: approximations indicate that it could have been around 60 to 70lb at 24inches.

Making a Holmegaard style bow: hints

1. I recommend you start with your stave about 2 inches longer than your ideal bowlength and mark/cut the change in profile accordingly (i.e. further towards the nock), this will allow you to work this critical point back down the limb during tillering as you shorten the bow. Leave the 'outboard' end of the limbs wider than the dimensions given if you are of a cautious nature!
2. Tiller the bow very carefully: the deeper profile to the outer part of the limb means you may initially have the stave bending disproportionately near the handle, but as long as this is not overdone it's not a problem because of the wide, flat design of this section.
3. Leave plenty of wood in the handle to start with, gradually reducing this and the outboard section of the limbs as you increase the bend on the tiller.
4. The narrow, deep nock follows the bow's principle design advantage of reducing mass at the end of the limbs. If you use elm or any other soft timber the string can crush the wood on the back, so the extra depth of material also helps with this.

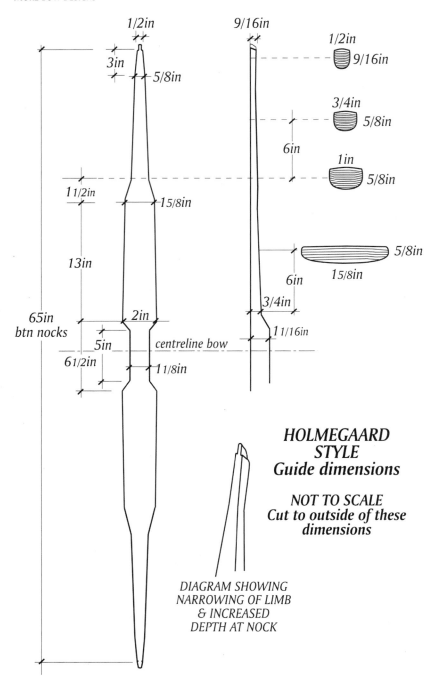

1/2in

9/16in

3in

5/8in

1/2in
9/16in

3/4in
5/8in

6in

1in
5/8in

1 1/2in

15/8in

5/8in
15/8in

13in

6in

3/4in

65in
btn nocks

2in

1 1/16in

5in

centreline bow

6 1/2in

1 1/8in

**HOLMEGAARD
STYLE
Guide dimensions**

*NOT TO SCALE
Cut to outside of these
dimensions*

*DIAGRAM SHOWING
NARROWING OF LIMB
& INCREASED
DEPTH AT NOCK*

10. MAKING A HORN THUMBRING

There are various ways of loosing a bowstring: the three-fingered loose was considered a 'new-fangled' invention in parts of England during mediaeval times, the two-fingered (Flemish) draw being a common technique. The simple 'pinch' grip using the thumb and index finger is still used by some native American traditional archers, and photographs of Ishi, the last Yahi indian, show him using this technique with his arrow rested on the thumb of his bowhand —shooting the arrow from what is considered by many western archers as technically the 'wrong' side of the bow. I would not encourage you to try using a thumbring with an English longbow, (in any case it isn't historically accurate) nor any bow where the bowyer is likely to have strong objections. If, however, you have a relatively short bow and perhaps are struggling with string pinch, or possess a suitable Asian style bow, or just want to have fun with a bow you have made yourself, this is yet another aspect of traditional archery you can enjoy!

The 'thumb lock'

The string is held in the joint of the thumb with the index and, in some versions, the adjacent finger hooked over the thumb; for a really secure lock the thumb should be crooked sufficiently around the string to press into the third finger. The arrow rests lightly against the knuckle of the index finger as illustrated.

Variations of the thumblock have been used in Asia for thousands of years. It provides a strong grip on the string during draw, but will feel unfamiliar at first, particularly to archers used to a finger loose; take your time to practice ensuring you are in a safe situation in case the string slips.

The use of a thumb-lock allows the arrow to be loosed from either side of the bow, although you may need to decide which side to stick to for consistency. There are advantages to shooting from off the thumb of the bowhand, particularly for horsearchers who might find the arrow being blown off the knuckle with the forward movement of the horse at speed.

Some form of protection for the thumb is essential —Japanese archers developed the shooting glove, for instance. The thumbring has been used for centuries and there are many finely decorated and beautiful thumbrings from Eastern cultures in Museums and private collections. Thumbrings can be made from any suitably tough material which can be shaped —leather, bone, stone, brass, silver and horn are all suitable, and in the past precious stones such as jade were used; some rings were inlaid with precious metals and beautifully carved. There are various shapes of thumbring (some are illustrated later) and you may like to experiment to find which type you prefer. To try out the thumbblock initially you could make a simple thumb flap from leather (similar to the finger tab) and if you enjoy shooting this style, a well-fitted horn or bone thumbring is advisable; with a little effort you can make one which fits you perfectly.

Fitting

It is useful to know how the thumbring is fitted before you start making one; firstly the ring is placed on the thumb at 90 degrees to the final position (A). It is then turned to cover the pad of the thumb. (B)

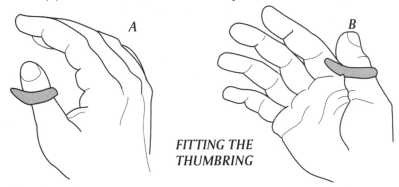

FITTING THE THUMBRING

Main points to note are:
  – the fit is important, it should be comfortable, but not too loose; you may need more than one try to get the ideal fit
  – correct fit helps ensure a secure (and safe) lock
  – the ring should protect the joint and the pad of the thumb and fit the contour of the thumb perfectly
  – too loose, and you will not have a secure lock and the ring may fly off on loosing; it will also be painful to use
  – too tight and it will be not only be painful, it can cut off the blood supply which is not conducive to a good release!
  – test the ring before finishing, it may seem a comfortable fit until you come to use it for any length of time.

Method

1. Cut a piece of horn with one flat side, and one side angled as illustrated.
2. Sand or file the external surfaces to the approximate finished size, leaving 2mm all round for final shaping and adjustment.
3. Drill the start of the thumb hole: I started with a 16mm diameter bit, but this will depend on your thumb size and shape, in any case allow plenty of material on the piece for filing and sanding to a perfect fit.

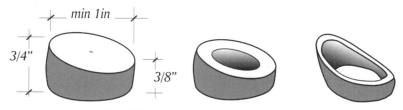

STAGES IN MAKING A THUMBRING

4. Using a round or half-round file, carefully enlarge the thumb hole and shape the lip, regularly test-fitting it over the thumb as described above: the hole should be oval, and the ring should be a tight but comfortable fit, with the inside of the protective lip fitting the contours of the thumb exactly. It must be long enough to protect the pad of the thumb without getting in the way of the locking fingers or affecting the clean loose of the string.

5. Remove material to form your preferred final shape. Before finishing, you may find it useful to test draw your bow using the ring. The lip should be smooth and rounded to allow the string to slip cleanly over it once the lock is released.

6. Polish the ring with increasingly fine abrasives and steel wool, ensuring there are no sharp corners or rough edges.

| *1. With groove for string* | *2. Turkish style thumbring with 'kulak'* | *3. Cylindrical with lip to hold string* |

DIFFERENT SHAPES OF THUMBRING

Variations

You may like to file a groove as illustrated (type 2)or form a lip as in type 3 to hold the string if you feel this is more secure. For comfort you could line the ring with leather, or add a flap of leather (*'kulak'*) to protect the inside of your thumb, particularly at the joint where it can get a bit tender! Note: the string should rest on the lip of the thumbring, not the leather.

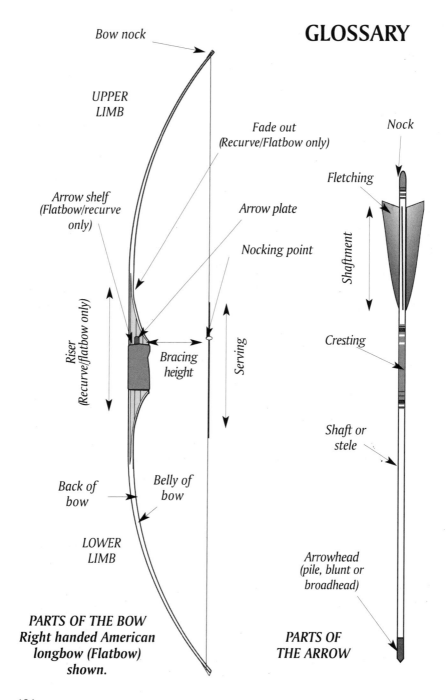

GLOSSARY

Bow nock

UPPER
LIMB

Fade out
(Recurve/Flatbow only)

Arrow shelf
(Flatbow/recurve
only)

Arrow plate

Nocking point

*Riser
(Recurve/flatbow only)*

*Bracing
height*

Serving

Back of
bow

Belly of
bow

LOWER
LIMB

Nock

Fletching

Shaftment

Cresting

*Shaft or
stele*

*Arrowhead
(pile, blunt or
broadhead)*

PARTS OF THE BOW
Right handed American
longbow (Flatbow)
shown.

*PARTS OF
THE ARROW*

American longbow	(aka in England as American flatbow or AFB). Has a rectangular limb section and deep, narrow handle.
Anchor	Part of face where drawing hand is located at full draw.
Angular bow	Bow with '<' profile: e.g. as pictured in Assyrian reliefs (c.800 BC)
Arrow plate	Protective plate on longbow which prevents chafing at the point where the arrow passes.
Arrow rake	Small 'rake' used for searching for arrows in long grass and undergrowth.
Arrow rest	An artificial projection to assist in consistent location of the arrow. (Usually used on recurves)
Arrow slap	When arrow hits the side of bow on release.
Ascham	A traditional longbow storage cabinet, named after the tutor of Elizabeth the First and author of "Toxophilus".
Atl-atl	Throwing stick used to cast fletched darts.
Back	Side of the bow facing away from the archer.
Backing	Material laminated onto the back of the bow.
Barb	As in 'barbed and tanged' arrowhead: projections to resist extraction of arrowhead, sim. broadheads.
Barebow	Class of shooting without sights.
Barred	Of fletching: from particular breeds of turkey; artificially dyed & barred feathers are also available.
Barrelled	An arrow shaft which is tapered 'fore and aft' (see also 'chested' & 'bobtailed').
Belly	Side of the bow facing the archer.
Billet	Piece of wood from which a bow can be made.
BL-BS	British Long-Bow Society.
Bloom	Repair of bow: usually layers of wood laid into belly.
Bludgeon	Another name for a blunt or small game head.
Blunt	Type of arrow head used for roving or small game hunting, can be metal or rubber.
Bobtailed	An arrow with the shaft tapered toward the nock.
Bodkin	An armour/mail piercing warhead; varies from 1/2in. to 4 inches long. (See also 'Type10')
Boss	Arrow-stopping part of target, to which target face is fixed.
Boughstave	Bow stave (usually yew) from limb or branch of the tree.
Bouncer	Arrow which fails to stick in the target. Rules vary regarding scoring of 'witnessed' bouncers according to organisation running the competition.
Bowhand	The hand which holds the bow.
Bowsling	A strap preventing bow from falling from archer's grasp on loosing (more commonly found in target styles).
Bowstave	A billet trimmed to make a bow.
Bow-window	Area of riser cut away to assist target/sight relationship.
Bowyer's float	(Old E: 'flote') A version of the toothed hand tool which is specifically used by bowmakers and which is generally curved in shape to avoid gouging.

105

Bowyer's knot	Also known as the timber hitch, used to tie the bottom of the traditional string on a longbow.
Brace	To string the bow.
Bracer	Armguard. Protects the bow arm if hit by the string.
Bracing height	Distance between bow and string when braced.
Breasted	An arrow shaft which is tapered 'fore and aft', with the thickest part towards the fletched end. (Also 'chested')
Brush button	A rubber button which touches the belly. This prevents brush catching at this point, and can also assist silencing by reducing the sound of string slap.
Bullet point	Type of target pile of rounded conical shape.
Butt (Mediaeval).	Traditionally a mound of earth placed behind practice targets
Butt bow	Relatively light draw weight longbow for target use.
Button nock	Simple nock without a groove which the string loop slips over, or is knotted around.
Cable-backed	(Of bow): bow with tightened sinew or similar cable on the back. (As Inuit and Siberian traditional bows)
Cant	Shooting with the bow at an angle off the vertical.
Carriage bow	A take apart longbow, jointed in the handle.
Cast	Ability of bow to discharge the arrow.
Centre-shot	Bows which allow the arrow to pass bow near its centreline by use of a cutaway in the riser section.
Chisel pile	Arrow head with conical point.
Chrysal	Collapsing of wood fibres on belly of a bow, due to compression. (Also 'fret')
Clocking	Assessment of arrows by shooting and registering differences in flight, this helps achieve a matched set.
Clothyard	Historic measurement of arrow shafts. Exact measure disputed, generally thought to be in 37in.
Clout	A target (originally a cloth) used for long distance shooting.
Composite bow	Bow made from laminations of dissimilar materials.
Cock feather	Fletching which is at right angles to the nock.
Compass	A longbow will 'come compass' if it is tillered to form an arc when full drawn.
Conical pile	Arrow head with conical point. (Also 'chisel')
Core	Wooden part of composite/backed bow.
Creep	Tendency to let arrow edge forward after achieving full draw and just before loose. (Poor technique)
Cresting	Coloured bands around breast of arrow shaft to indicate ownership.
Critical	Said of a bow which sacrifices stability for speed.
Crown dipping	Dipped application of paint to shaftment.
Cutaway	Area of riser cut out to form sight window.
Dead loose	Too gradual a relaxation of the drawing hand, robbing the bow of cast. (See 'lively' or 'sharp' loose)
Deal	An historic classification of timber by size (usually pine or spruce varieties): 9in x 2in. x 41/2in.

Deflex	Where the bow limbs bend towards the belly near the handle.
Deflex-reflex	Found in modern flatbow design: unbraced limbs deflex toward archer at handle, then reflex away towards tips.
Dips	These markedly deepen the section of a longbow approx. 2in. from the handle. A (Victorian) development.
Draw(ing) hand	Hand that pulls the string.
Dribber	An inaccurate archer. (Mediaeval)
Dry loose	Releasing the string without an arrow on it. Will seriously damage a bow. (Also 'dry-release')
Ear	Stiff section at end of limb to composite bow. (*Turk: 'siyah'*)
Earlywood (springwood)	Part of cross sectional growth rings indicating early growth in spring. Generally a weak layer.
EFAA	English Field Archery Association.
Elliptical tiller	Bow profile with a degree of bend through the handle.
End	A set number of arrows shot before scoring. (Usually three for traditional longbow rounds, otherwise six)
Endless string	Where strands of string are continuously looped to form the main body of the string.
Fade-out	Most slender part of riser at start of bow limb.
Fast	Warning cry to stop shooting
Field pile	Arrowhead with 'waisted' point, intended to reduce arrow penetration. (Also 'long-nosed')
Field shooting	A form of archery where a course is set out in open ground and woodland with targets at various distances.
Fishtailing	An arrow is said to 'fishtail' when flailing from side to side in flight.
Fistmele	A traditional way of checking bracing height by using the clenched fist with an extended thumb.
Flatbow	A bow with straight limbs of wide, thin section.
Flemish loose	Two fingered draw.
Flemish string	Traditional string where strands of string material are cut to length and loops formed by 'laying-in'.
Fletching	Specifically a feather cut to shape to maintain steady arrow flight.
Flight shooting	Shooting an arrow to achieve maximum distance.
Floor tiller	Method of assessing a bow limbs curvature and flexibility by resting the nock on the floor applying pressure to the handle.
Flu-Flu	An arrow with a large area of fletching (or spirally fletched) to slow down flight. Used for roving.
Follow through	Maintaining stance ('form') after loosing.
Follow the string	A bow is said to do this if it takes a permanent curvature towards the string when unbraced.
Footing/footed	Hardwood spliced onto the head of an arrow shaft to strengthen the weakest point behind the pile.
Force-draw	A force draw curve is plotted on a graph (draw length to draw weight) in order to assess the dynamics of bow.

Forward loose	Releasing the arrow before full draw is achieved.
Forgiving	Said of a bow which reduces the effects of archer's inconsistencies in shooting.
Forker	Forked arrowhead traditionally used for small game.
Fret	Another word for 'chrysal'. (Collapse of wood fibre on belly of bow)
Gadding	Erratic flight of arrow.
Gap-shooting	Method of aiming using sight window of bow or pile of arrow as an elementary form of sight.
GNAS	Grand National Archery Society.
Grain	Alignment of fibres on vertical axis of log.
Green (of wood)	Unseasoned timber.
Green (of archer)	Unseasoned toxophilite.
Grey goosewing	Traditional fletching of the mediaeval archer and the stuff of romance.
Growth ring	Layers of early and latewood (spring and summer growth respectively), making up the yearly growth of the tree.
Hand bow	Not a crossbow: requires more skill from the archer to draw and shoot.
Hanger	Arrow which fails to adequately penetrate the boss and hangs across the target face.
Heavy bow	A bow of high draw weight. (i.e. not weight-in-hand)
Helical fletch	Where fletching is twisted around the shaft, rather than merely angled.
Hoyles	Short range natural marks in roving (molehills, tufts of grass).
Hysteresis	Difference (loss) of energy between that stored at full draw and that imparted to the arrow.
Instinctive	Said of an archer who shoots without consciously taking aim.
Judo point	Special tined and sprung arrowhead for use when roving in long grass.
Knapping	Working flint to form sharp edged tools, and arrowheads
Kulak (*Turkish*)	Leather flap on thumbring to protect inside of joint.
Kyudo	Traditional Japanese archery, a samurai skill developed in the early mediaeval period.
Laid-in	e.g. loops of a 'Flemish' string which are corded into the main hank of string material.
Latewood	Stronger, more dense part of growth ring (see 'earlywood').
'Leaf' head	Simple stone arrowpoint. (Neolithic). Variant: 'lozenge' shape. Also shape of bronze arrowheads, usually tanged.
Limb	As in 'top' ('upper') limb and bottom ('lower') limb of bow.
Leak	(Of target) weak point where arrow passes straight through the boss.
Longbow	Generally said of a bow that is over 5ft long, straight limbed and of a 'D' or rounded 'D' section in UK.
Long-nosed	Of pile: another name for field pile.
Loose	The action of releasing the string.
Low fletched	Having short fletchings of shallow profile.

Mark	Any target or object at which an archer shoots.
Master eye	Dominant eye which controls aiming. Not necessarily the same as the dominant hand.
Mediterranean loose	Three fingered draw, index finger above nock.
Millen-cut file or 'millenicut'	A toothed file very useful to the bowmaker.
Needle bodkin	Long bodkin (sim. London Museum Type 10).
NFAS	National Field Archery Society.
Nock	1. Of bow: string grooves at limb tips, either reinforced with horn or hardwood, or 'self' nocked. 2. Of arrow: groove for string at end of shaft, usually plastic, or self-nocked, possibly reinforced.
Nocking point	Place on string where arrow must be consistently placed in order to maintain accuracy. Usually reinforced with thread.
Off the shelf	Shooting with the arrow resting on the shelf of the bow cutaway, i.e. without a separate arrow rest.
Overbowed	Said of an archer with a bow with too high a draw weight.
Overdraw	1. To draw a bow beyond its designed draw length. 2. To draw the arrow inside the belly of the bow.
Overhand	Where the target is sighted over the bow hand at full draw. (Also 'forehand')
Overstrung	Too high a bracing height.
Paddle bow	Wide limbed bow with broadest section at about mid-limb.
Parabolic	Of fletching shape, curved profile.
Petals	Thin layers of wood laid into bow as a patch repair to form a 'bloom'.
Piece	Patch, bloom or splice to bow as repair. Also as in 'piece' bow where apprentices made bows from offcuts/rejects to prove their skill. Also footing: 'pieced shaft'
Pike	(Old E: pyke) To shorten a longbow, to increase draw weight.
Pile	A cylindrical arrowhead with no cutting edges. Usually with a tapered or parallel socket to fit the shaft.
Pinching	Forcing of draw fingers onto nock by acute angle of string —can cause the arrow to come off the rest.
Plucking	Said of a loose where the string is released with a sideways plucking action, causing erratic arrow flight.
Point blank	Distance where point-of-aim and the mark are the same.
Point-of-aim	Place where the archer locates the tip of his arrow in order to achieve correct cast for hitting the mark.
Popinjay	Type of shooting where special blunt arrows are loosed vertically at targets on a 90ft high mast.
Porpoising	Said of arrows where nock dips and rises in flight.
Primary loose	Simple thumb and index finger draw.
Pyramid bow	Wide limbed bow with broadest section near handle.
Quiver	Arrow container used when shooting, from french 'cuivre'.
Recurve	Curvature at bow tips away from archer.

Reflex	Said of limbs which curve away from the belly of a bow (i.e. opposite way to direction when strung).
Release	Action of releasing string. (Also 'loose')
Riser	Central, handle section of a bow.
Roving	Traditionally, shooting at natural marks, the closest to the mark naming the next.
Run on the bow	Said of a fletching which touches the bow on loosing and which can be subsequently damaged.
Serving	Reinforcing thread 'whipped' onto string at points of wear.
Set	Permanent curvature of an unbraced bow towards the string.
Shaft	Main body of an arrow (in traditional terms the or the wooden part) whole arrow.
Shaftment	Part of the arrow occupied by the fletchings.
Sharp	Said of a quick action at loosing.
Shelf	'Ledge' formed in bow riser to form lower part of sight window (or cutaway in flatbow or recurve) which can be used as the arrow rest, as in 'shooting off the shelf'.
Shield	Traditional fletching shape.
Short-nosed	Of pile –also chisel point i.e. with conical end.
Sight window	Cut away portion of bow riser which allows for centre- or near centre-shooting of arrows.
Sinew	Tendons: for a bow the back or leg tendons of large animals such as deer, antelope or buffalo are preferred.
Siyahs ('Ears')	Stiffened sections at limb ends of Turkish composite bow
Slashing	Of loose –a sharp backward plucking action during the loose generally deliberately used in flight shooting.
Snap shooting	To shoot prematurely with a too-rapid loose. (Deliberate style for trick shooting)
SPTA	Society for the Promotion of Traditional Archery.
Spine	Flexibility of the arrow shaft, usually measured in lbs over 26in. length (wooden arrows).
Spine tester	Graduated device for testing the spine of shafts.
Stability	Required of a bow to assist consistent accurate shooting: a function of manageable speed, lack of kick or torque etc.
Stack-bellied	Said of a longbow with a deep arched 'D' section ('stacked')
Stand in	An arrow strong enough to withstand the energy imparted on loosing the bow is said to 'stand in' well.
Stave	Unworked piece of wood suitable for arrow or bow.
Stacking	Said of a bow which requires a disproportionate increase in effort towards the end of the draw.
Stele	Traditional word for the wooden shaft of an arrow.
Straight-staved	Said of a bow with straight limbs with no recurve.
String silencers	Fitted to quieten string noise (usually recurves).
Stringer	Corded device to facilitate stringing a bow and avoid damage due to twisting the limbs.
String keep	Cord or ribbon tied to top nock, or leather band on the top limb: prevents string from coming off the unbraced bow.

String walking	Changing the position of the draw hand on the string in order to modify cast/trajectory.
Superglue	Cyanoacrylate ester glue of high bond.
Swallowtail	Large broadhead with sweeping barbs which increase the cutting edges for shooting large game etc.
Tab	Simple protection to string fingers.
Take down	Usually a recurved bow with limbs which are detachable from the riser. (Also 'take-apart')
Tang	Projection on arrowhead for fixing to shaft.
Tassel	Woollen arrow cleaner suspended from an archer's belt.
Tertiary loose	Where the thumb, index and middle fingers are used to draw the string.
Throw one's arm	The sideways pushing away of the bow on release.
Thumbring	Made of horn metal, bone or leather, protects the thumb when using the Asian thumblock release.
Thumb-lock	Method of gripping the string, usually using a thumbring or glove, where the thumb is locked in place round the string with the index finger.
Tiller	1. Bowyer's equipment: for assessing curvature of bow during manufacture. 2. Difference in bow to string distance should one limb be stronger (usually the lower limb).
Timber hitch	Adjustable knot used to tie the lower loop of a.Flemish string on a longbow. (Also 'bowyer's knot')
Toggle	Special tool for twisting cord fitted to cable backed bows.
Torque	Natural inclination of a bow to twist in the hand on release.
'Type 10 '	Small bodkin.
'Type 16'	Small broadhead. (Classification of arrowhead types by London Museum).
Underbowed	Said of an archer who has too light a bow, resulting in poor technique.
Understrung	Too low a bracing height.
Upshot	Gained by the archer closest to the mark when roving.
Underhand	Shooting when point of aim is under the bowhand at full draw (e.g. as in long-range shooting).
Vanes	Originally applied to fletchings, but now more usually applied to the plastic items.
Wand	Where a vertical stick forms the mark.
War bow	Heavy draw weight longbow for shooting 'military' arrows.
Whip-ended	1. Bow where the ends of the limbs bend predominantly. 2. Old term for recurved ends to longbows.
Weight-in-hand	Actual physical weight of a bow.
Whistler	Arrow with special head designed to whistle as it flies.
Yumi	Traditional Japanese longbow, laminated and up to 8 ft long.

USEFUL DATA/REFERENCE

WEIGHTS
15.432 grains =1 gramme
1 oz (avoir) =28.35 grammes
1oz. (troy) =31.1 grammes
1lb = 0.4536 kg
1 kilo = 2.205lb

Old arrow measures (silver coin)
1 silver penny =7.26 Grains (approx.)
12 silver pennies (d) =1 shilling (s)

Coinage	Grains
2s 0d	174.4
2s 3d	196.2
2s 6d	218.0
2s 9d	239.8
3s 0d	261.36
3s 3d	283.2
3s 6d	305.2
4s 0d	348.8 etc.

Hence a 'five shilling arrow' would weigh 436 grains (approx. 28.25grammes).

LENGTH
1/16 inch=1.59mm
1/8 inch=3.175mm
1 inch =2.544 centimetres
1 foot=30.53 centimetres
1 yard =91.48 centimetres
1 metre = 3.281 feet

ENGLISH LONGBOWS
Basis for all UK Societies classification, based on British Long-Bow Society (BL-BS) specification. (2002 rulebook).
Materials: can be laminated, 'self' or backed, made from wood. Bamboo is permitted.
Limb section: depth to be no less than 5/8 of width at any point.
Length: not less than 60" between nocks for arrows less than 27", no less than 66" for 27" or longer arrows.
No arrow support permitted other than the hand.
Horn nocks are required except for flight and roving events.

STANDARD ARROW (BL-BS Specification, 2002)
Min. weight 52 grammes overall. Shaft: Ash or sim. 3/8" diameter, length 31 1/2" from base of nock to shoulder of head. Fletching min. 6" at shaftment, to stand min. 3/4" off shaft at highest point. Fit with bodkin (type 10*) or broadhead: (type 15* large or type 16* small).
*London Museum classification for arrowheads.

Full specifications and Rules of Shooting are available from the British Long-Bow Society.

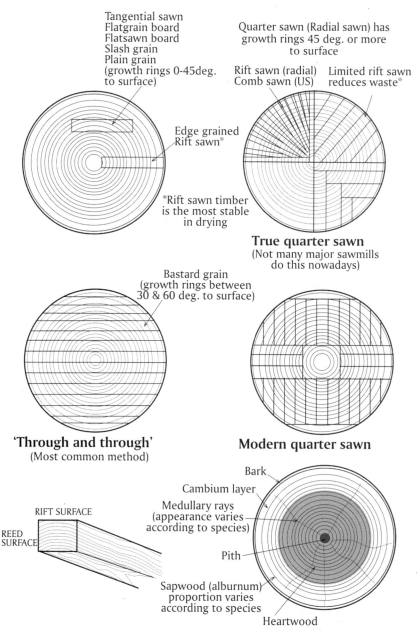

Tangential sawn
Flatgrain board
Flatsawn board
Slash grain
Plain grain
(growth rings 0-45deg.
to surface)

Quarter sawn (Radial sawn) has
growth rings 45 deg. or more
to surface

Rift sawn (radial)   Limited rift sawn
Comb sawn (US)   reduces waste*

Edge grained
Rift sawn*

*Rift sawn timber
is the most stable
in drying

True quarter sawn
(Not many major sawmills
do this nowadays)

Bastard grain
(growth rings between
30 & 60 deg. to surface)

'Through and through'
(Most common method)

Modern quarter sawn

Bark

Cambium layer

Medullary rays
(appearance varies
according to species)

RIFT SURFACE

REED
SURFACE

Pith

Sapwood (alburnum)
proportion varies
according to species

Heartwood

SOME UK & US CUT TIMBER REFERENCES
cross section (transverse) plane of log

INDEX

A

Adhesives
    backings 72
    bows 72
    fletching 37, 41
    footings/self nocks 43
    hide glue 82
    nocking point 20
    piles 36, 41
    serving 58
American longbow (AFB)
    4 et seq., 14
    deflex/reflex 4-5
    making 64 et seq..
Archer's paradox 2-3, 18, 25
Armguard 23
Arrows 24 et seq.
    care 45
    fit to string 21, 42, 59
    flu-flu 45
    heads 36
    length/spine 28
    making 37 et seq.
    repairs 45
    spine 19, 25 et seq.
    storage 46
    straightening 45
    weight 19, 30
    centre of balance 28
Arrow care 45
Arrow plate 23, 82
Arrow rests 21
Arrow shelf 2, 21

B

Backings 5, 62, 64, 67, 75
    rawhide 73, 82
Bamboo (cane) 69, 113
Barrelled shaft 28, 40 *(ill.)*
Billet size 70 et seq.
Binding (fletching) 43
Blunts 36
Bobtailed shaft 40 *(ill.)*

Bois d'arc 70
Bound nocks 42
Bound fletchings 43
Bow design 64 et seq.
Bow length
    longbow 11
    American l/bow(AFB) 15
    recurve 16
Bowmaker (finding/choosing) 10
Bow profile 13
Bow draw weight
    to spine 26
Bow windows 6
Bow woods 10, 69
Bowyer's hitch 51
Bracers 23
Bracing height 19, 34, 41, 59
    marking arrows for 41
Breaking strain 50
Breasted shaft 40 *(ill.)*
    flight arrow 47
British Long-Bow Society 11, 35, 113
Broadheads, 13, 34, 43
Bullet point 36
Butt bow 13

C

Cable-backed bows 94 et seq.
Cane 69, 113
Care of bows 59 et seq.
Cast 1
Centreline of bows 13, 14, 15
Centre-shot bows 2, 4
Chested shaft 40, for flight 46
Chrysal 61
Clout shooting 30, 35
    arrows for 30, 35
Cock feathers 34 *(ill.)* 42
Coinage (weights) 112
'Compass' (of bow) *13 (ill.)*, 14
Competitions 11 et seq.
    arrows for 34
Conical pile 36

Conversions (weight/length) 112
Cording (strings) 54
Craft Guild 9
Cresting 40, 41
Crown dipping (shafts) 41
Cutaway 2, 6
Cutting
    stave 76
    fletching 31

D
Dacron 50
Degreasing 72
Dimensions
    Cable bow 96
    English longbow 87
    Flatbow 86
    Holmegaard 100
    Meare Heath 92
    Pyramid bow 88
Dipping (arrow shafts) 41
Dips (bow) 14
Dominant eye 11, 17
Draw length 10, 15, 66
Draw weight 11, 12, 15,26, 66, 80
Dry-loosing 47, 59
Dyneema 50

E
Elliptical tiller 79
Endless string 51

F
Fast flight 50
Feathers 30
    cock- 34, 42
    dyeing 32
    flight arrow 48
    left/right wing 32, 33
    reshaping 34
    trimming 31
    waterproofing 32
Field shooting 10
    arrows for 32

Finishes
    general 9, 63, 73
    natural 83
Fishtail joints 75
Fistmele *19(ill.)* 20
Flatbow
    GRP: ordering 14
    'self': making 64 et seq
Flemish string 51
Fletching 30 et seq.
    flight arrows 48
    helical 33,34
    jig *32 (ill.)*
    left/right wing 32, 36
    making 31
    oil line 30
    reshaping 34
    'running the bow' 34
    shapes 33, 38
    size/flight 33, 48

Flight shooting 12, 48
    arrows for 30, 47
    bows for 12
    strings for 20, 52
Flu-Flu 45
Footings 43
Frets (chrysals) 61

G
Gap shooting 6-7
Gloves, shooting 27
Glues
    backings 68, 77
    fletching 36, 40
    general 68, 72
    footings/self nocks 43
    serving 58
Grain
    arrows 19, 24, 30
    bow woods 70, 71
    direction 65
Grains (weight) 19, 30, 112
Green wood 68, 90

Grey Goosewing 30
Grip 15, 16, 85
GRP 4

H
Handle
        joints 75
        packing 85
        finish 83, 85
'Heavy' arrows 13
Heavy draw weight bows 12, 13
Helical fletch 33, 34
Hemp (strings) 50
Hide glue 82
Hitch 46
Holding 11, 50, 59
Holmegaard bow 99et seq.
Horn bow nocks 84
Horn inserts (nocks) 42
Horn thumbring 23
        making 101 et seq.

I
Instinctive shooting 1, 8, 18

J
Judo point 35, 36, 43

K
Kevlar 50
Knots
        cordage 97
        hitch 51
Kilo (conversions) 112

L
Laid-in string 49 et seq.
Laminated bows 8, 64
Length
        bow 5, 10, 14, 93
        arrow 19, 27
Lift (backing) 61
Limb design 1, 2, 5, 65, 66
Limb tiller 77
Linen

strings 50
cordage bow 95
Longbow (English)
        BL-BS spec. 9
        care of 59
        'compass' 13
        making 83
        ordering 9
        selection 9
        target style 14
        tillered profile 13, 69
        tillering 77
        reflexed 1, 15
        woods 10,
Loops (string) 54, 84
Loose 101

M
Maintenance
        bows 61 et seq.
        arrows 45
Marking out (bow) 76
Mary Rose 14
Master eye 11, 17
Matching equipment 18, 24, 26
Materials
        arrows 4
        bowmaking 67.
        strings 50
Meare Heath bow 91et seq.
Mediterranean loose 59
Moisture content
        arrow wood 24
        boards for bows 68
        timber for bows 89

N
Nocks (arrow)
        bound 42 *(ill.)*
        fit to string 22, 42
        inserts 42
        loops to fit 54
        removal 46
        self 42, 60

Nocks(bow) 10, 75 et seq.
       string loop 54
Nocking point
       adjusting 21 *(ill.)*
       location 20
       materials 21
       temporary 58
Nock sets 21

O
'Off-the-hand' 21
Off-the-shelf shooting 16, 21
Oil line (feather) 30
Ordering (bow) 10 et seq.
Overdrawing 53

P
Paddle bow 66
Parabolic fletching 33
Paradox 2-3 *(ill.)*
Penobscot bow 6 *(ill.)*
Piles
       parallel fit 41
       pinning 41
Pistol grip 15
Plastic nocks 36
       adjusting fit 22 *(ill.)*
       fitting 39
       removing 46
Point blank 8
Polishing nocks 85
Port Orford Cedar 24
'Primitive' bows
       definition 59, 65
       making 64 et. seq.
Pyramid bow 66

Q
Quartersawn 113
Quivers 49

R
Rawhide 4,73
Recurve 4, 5

Reflexing jig 95
Rests (arrow) 2
Riser 1
Roving 12, 32
Roving marks 7, 12
       arrows for 35
Running the bow 34
Running repairs 63

S
Sapwood 67, 89
Self bows 10, 64
Self nocks
       bows 12, 81
       arrows 22, 42
Serving 20, 56 et seq.
Serving tool 56
'Set' 9, 62
Shafts
       footing 44
       grain 24
       making 25
       materials 24
       shapes 24
       spine 25
       straightening 45
Sheaf arrow 35
Shelf (arrow) 2, 21
Shield fletching 33
Shooting gloves 23
Shoulder nock 81
Sight windows 6
Sinew backings 4, 5, 73
Spine (arrow shaft) 19, 25
       adjustments 27
       English longbow 26, 62
       graph 27
       incorrect 26
       measuring 26
       rule of thumb 26
Spine tester 27
Splitting timber 90
Stacking 5, 11, 15
'Standard' arrow 12, 112

Static recurve 5
Stele shapes 40 *(ill.)*
Storage
    arrows 45
    longbows/self bows 62
    recurve/AFB 63
String follow 57
    avoiding 55
Strings 20
    loops 54, 84
    making 50 et seq.
    materials 50-51, 93
    number of strands 20, 52
    waxing 58
Stringers 59, 60, 63
Stringing 60 *(ill.)*
Stringwalking 59
String follow 9, 62

T
Tabs 23
Take apart (Take down) bows 5, 16
Target shooting 10
    arrows for 31
Tassel 45
Test shooting 80
Thumbring 23, 26
    making 101
    fitting 102 *(ill.)*
Thumblock 108
Tiller (tool) 72
Tiller (bow) 62, 80
Tillered profile
    English longbow 13
    general 7, 72 et seq
Tillering 77 et seq
Timbers
    arrows 24
    bows 67
    buying 70
    terms 113
Timber hitch 51
Toggle (cable bow) 95

Tools (bowmaking) 74
Traditional (definition) 1
Tuning 18 et seq.
Twisting (limbs) 62, 77, 79
Types of bow
    Cable 94
    English longbow 1-2
    Flatbow/American
        longbow 4
    Paddle 66
    Pyramid 66
    recurve 4

U
Units of weight 112
    grains (conversion) 112

W
'War' arrows 13
War bow 2, 13
Waterproofing
    fletchings 32
    tabs 23
Waxing string 58
Weight-in-hand 16
Windows (bow) 2, 6, 16
    gap shooting and 8 *(ill.)*
Wood (bows) 67
Working recurve 5

Y
Yew 10, 70
Yew self bows 8, 10, 51, 54, 59, 67

NOTES

NOTES

NOTES

NOTES